TRANSFORMING STATE
RESPONSES TO FEMINICIDE

PERSPECTIVES ON CRIME, LAW AND JUSTICE IN THE GLOBAL SOUTH

Series editors: Prof Kerry Carrington and Prof Máximo Sozzo

Scholarly perspectives on crime, law and justice have generally been sourced from a select number of countries from the Global North, whose journals, conferences, publishers and universities dominate the intellectual landscape. As a consequence, research about these matters in the Global South has tended to uncritically reproduce concepts and arguments developed in the Global North to understand local problems and processes. In recent times, there have been substantial efforts to undo this colonized way of thinking leading to a burgeoning body of new work. Southern theories, subaltern knowledges and border epistemologies are challenging the social science to open up new ways of thinking about society, crime, law and justice.

This book series aims to publish and promote innovative new scholarship with a long term view of enhancing cognitive justice and democratising the production of knowledge. Topics of interest from the perspective of the global south include - environmental and ecological plunder; gendered violence; religion, war and terror; drug wars; the historical and contemporary legacies of slavery; the contemporary legacies of injustice arising from dispossession and colonisation; systems of punishment and forms of customary or transitional justice; human rights abuses and struggles for justice - all of which threaten the security of peoples who inhabit the global south.

Previous Volume:

Southern Green Criminology: A Science to End Ecological Discrimination
Edited by David Rodríguez Goyes

Forthcoming Volumes:

Perspectives on the Histories of Punishment in Ireland
Edited by Lynsey Black, Louise Brangan and Deirdre Healy

TRANSFORMING STATE RESPONSES TO FEMINICIDE

Women's Movements, Law and Criminal Justice Institutions in Brazil

FIONA MACAULAY

University of Bradford, UK

United Kingdom – North America – Japan – India
Malaysia – China

Emerald Publishing Limited
Howard House, Wagon Lane, Bingley BD16 1WA, UK

First edition 2021

Reprints and permissions service
Contact: permissions@emeraldinsight.com

British Library Cataloguing in Publication Data
A catalogue record for this book is available from the British Library

ISBN: 978-1-80071-566-0 (Print)
ISBN: 978-1-80071-565-3 (Online)
ISBN: 978-1-80071-567-7 (Epub)

Printed and bound by CPI Group (UK) Ltd, Croydon, CR0 4YY

ISOQAR certified
Management System,
awarded to Emerald
for adherence to
Environmental
standard
ISO 14001:2004.

ISOQAR
REGISTERED
Certificate Number 1985
ISO 14001

INVESTOR IN PEOPLE

CONTENTS

LIST OF TABLES

GLOSSARY OF TERMS AND ABBREVIATIONS USED

bancada feminina	cross-party women's caucus in Brazilian legislatures
Belém do Pará Convention	Inter-American Convention on the Prevention, Punishment, and Eradication of Violence against Women
BO	Police incident report (*boletim de ocorrência*)
CCJ	Standing Committee on Constitution, Justice and Citizenship (*Comissão de Constituição, Justiça e Cidadania*)
CEDAW	UN Convention for the Elimination of all Forms of Discrimination Against Women
CEVID	Committee on Women and Domestic Violence (*Coordenadoria Estadual das Mulheres em Situação de Violência Doméstica e Familiar*)
CIM	Inter-American Commission of Women (*Comisión Interamericana de Mujeres*)
CNDM	National Council for Women's Rights (*Conselho Nacional dos Direitos da Mulher*)
CNJ	National Justice Council (*Conselho Nacional de Justiça*)
CNMP	National Prosecutor's Office Council (*Conselho Nacional do Ministério Público*)
DEAMs	Women's police stations (*Delegacias Especializadas no Atendimento à Mulher*)
delegacia	Police precinct (run by the civil police, for the investigation of crimes)
FBSP	Brazilian Forum on Public Safety (*Fórum Brasileiro de Segurança Pública*)
feminicide	the intentional killing of a girl or woman for reasons related to social norms around gender roles

homicídio privilegiado	mitigated homicide, voluntary manslaughter
homicídio qualificado	aggravated homicide
IACHR	Inter-American Commission on Human Rights
JECrims	Criminal misdemeanour courts (*Juizados Especiais Criminais*)
MESECVI	Follow-up Mechanism to the Belém do Pará Convention (*Mecanismo de Seguimiento de la Convención de Belém do Pará*)
Model Protocol	Latin American Model Protocol for the Investigation of Gender-related Killings of Women (femicide/feminicide)
MP	Public Prosecutor's office (*Ministério Público*)
MPU	urgent protection measure (*medida protetiva urgente*)
NGO	Non-governmental organisation
OAS	Organization of American States
Procuradoria da Mulher	Women's Advocacy Office in Congress
PT	Workers' Party (*Partido dos Trabalhadores*)
SPM	Special Secretariat for Policies for Women (*Secretaria Especial de Políticas para as Mulheres*)
STF	Federal Supreme Court (*Supremo Tribunal Federal*)
STJ	Supreme Court of Justice (*Superior Tribunal de Justiça*)
TJ	State-level appellate court (*Tribunal de Justiça*)
UN	United Nations
UNSR	United Nations Special Rapporteur on Violence against Women
UN Women	United Nations Entity for Gender Equality and the Empowerment of Women

MAP OF BRAZIL

Source: https://d-maps.com/carte.php?num_car=4845&lang=en

ACKNOWLEDGEMENTS

This book is dedicated to the many researchers, academics, and criminal justice system professionals across Brazil whose insights have informed this book. It is always a privilege to spend time talking to individuals who are on the front-line of making change happen and have dedicated their working lives to reducing fear and insecurity for ordinary Brazilians, especially women and girls. I am especially grateful to colleagues in the Brazilian Forum on Public Safety for their support and for their pioneering work transforming the quality of criminal justice data and of public policy on crime and violence.

Chapter One

FEMINICIDE AS A LATIN AMERICAN ISSUE

INTRODUCTION

'A woman has been found stabbed to death.' A headline, repeated, word for word, almost daily, in local newspapers right across Brazil, from north to south, from small towns in the interior to the largest cities.[1] Of all the forms of lethal violence, feminicide – that is, the intentional killing of a girl or woman, most often by a partner or member of her family and for reasons specifically related to social norms around gender roles – is one of the most persistent. It is a 'sticky' problem, resistant to all kinds of other violence- and crime-reduction measures, even in countries that pride themselves on gender equality, democracy, and social stability. In the United Kingdom, for instance, on average two women a week are killed by current or former intimate partners, a figure unchanged for a decade.[2] In contexts of violent conflict, high crime, and deep social and gender inequality the victimisation of women can skyrocket. Due to its size, Brazil has the greatest absolute number of feminicides in Latin America. In 2019, 3,730 women were murdered, of which 1,326 were registered by the police as feminicides (FBSP, 2020a, p. 116).

The phenomenon of feminicide (or femicide, as it is also known) grabbed global attention as millions of women poured out onto the streets in countries as diverse as France, Argentina, Peru, India, Mexico, and El Salvador protesting at state inaction (Heinrich Böll Stiftung, 2017). The display in public places of thousands of pairs of blood-red shoes symbolising the many victims, the circulation of hashtags on social media – *#NiUnaMenos* ('Not one fewer'), *#VivaNosQueremos* ('We want to stay alive'), and *#NoEstamosSolas* ('We are not alone) – and the placards held aloft with enlarged pictures of sisters, daughters, and friends lost to misogynistic violence prompted international organisations to move this issue up their list of priorities.[3] In particular, the murder of women was reframed as a human security concern, not just as a 'women's issue' or a human rights matter.

A number of regional and international security and development organisations, such as the Council of Europe, Organization for Security and Co-operation in Europe, and the United Nations (UN) Office on Drugs and Crime, recognised feminicide, and violence against women more broadly, as 'a global health problem of epidemic proportions',[4] and issued declarations, protocols, and even new hard law in the form of the 2011 Istanbul Convention.[5] They were following the lead of Latin America, which two decades earlier had produced the 1994 Inter-American Convention on the Prevention, Punishment, and Eradication of Violence against Women (known as the Belém do Pará Convention), the world's first legally binding regional instrument on this issue.

Although declarations and treaties are one thing, effective implementation is something else altogether. After Latin American women's groups and researchers mobilised and lobbied, highlighting persistent government negligence, in 2013, the UN issued the Vienna Declaration on Femicide. In 2014, UN Women and the Office of the High Commissioner for Human Rights launched the Latin American Model Protocol for the Investigation of Gender-related Killings of Women (femicide/feminicide) – hereafter 'Model Protocol' – in a bid to enhance the performance of the hemisphere's justice agencies in tackling a crime that appeared to be out of control.[6] They chose Brazil as the country in which to test this, not just due to its high number of feminicides, but also because of the actual and potential capacity of its justice system to devise constructive responses to this crime.

To date, the literature on feminicide in Latin America has focussed mainly on Mexico, especially Ciudad Juárez, and Central America and their contexts of chronic violence linked to gangs and organised crime, human trafficking, legacies of armed conflict, poor governance, and impunity (Carcedo, 2010; Monárrez, 2009; Rodríguez, Montané, & Pulitzer, 2008). However, Brazil's situation is very different. Its female homicide rate is lower than in Central America (4.7 per 100,000 in 2017 compared to 13.8 in El Salvador the same year).[7] Its feminicides are more ordinary than extraordinary, committed overwhelmingly by current or former intimate partners, and thus much of this book focusses on domestic violence. As such, the story told here of how Brazil's criminal justice agencies built new institutional architecture and devised better practices and procedures for addressing gender-based violence offers transferable lessons for countries facing similar challenges.

The major contribution of this book is its focus on the factors and processes that have induced different parts of the Brazilian state to act more effectively to secure justice for feminicide victims and reduce its incidence. This study examines a number of inter-locking drivers of institutional innovation and capacity building: legislation (content and process), political environment, strategic action by feminist activists, executive branch investment, leadership and entrepreneurship in the police and in justice agencies, horizontal policy transfer, and collaboration between the agencies of the justice system and with local women's networks. It also traces the multi-layered and multi-dimensional process by which this ensemble of elements came together, inside and outside the Brazilian criminal justice system, to transform approaches to understanding, detecting, prosecuting, and preventing feminicide. Transformation occurs, in this story, through informal alliances of interest involving feminist academics, non-governmental organisations (NGOs), local campaigners, bureaucrats within the state machineries for women, politicians, journalists, and criminal justice professionals. This study traces the process by which the practical building blocks for tackling both domestic violence and feminicide were put in place by many actors, local, national, and international, how spaces for change were identified or created, and how individuals and networks worked within those spaces to push forward legal, policy, and procedural changes.

In documenting how the women's movement was able to engage police and justice institutions that had previously been impermeable to its influence, the book contributes to a very current debate, and a well-established literature, about how women's movements in Latin America, and around the world, engage with diverse spaces of the state. It also speaks to comparative literatures on struggles around gender rights and law, on socio-legal theory in Latin America and beyond, and on gender-sensitive approaches to security-sector and justice-sector reform. By giving voice to the policy entrepreneurs who have driven change within police and judicial institutions, the book contributes both to feminist institutionalism as well as to the incipient field of Southern criminology, which draws attention to knowledge and new, effective practices produced in the Global South (Carrington, Hogg, & Sozzo, 2016). This challenges assumptions about policy transfer from the Global North, whilst attention to policy innovations blossoming outside the dominant metropolitan centres in Brazil also decentres the narrative about knowledge production within the country.

Most studies of feminicide have concentrated on explaining its causes and impacts. Few examine the responses of criminal justice agencies, which are assumed to be incompetent and to sustain impunity. Brazil's justice system is renowned for its slowness and inefficiency, and its police forces suffer from chronic problems of corruption, excessive use of force, poor co-ordination, lack of accountability, and a machista culture. But with over 600,000 state-level officers across the country, they are also diverse, especially now that more women than ever are joining their ranks. Whilst their priorities and approaches vary enormously, one of their most routine duties is dealing with domestic violence. Back in the 1980s, under women's movement pressure on gender-based violence, the civil police instituted the pioneering women's police stations (*Delegacias Especializadas no Atendimento à Mulher* – DEAMs). These generated global interest and emulation, and studies of their origins and functioning (Hautzinger, 2007; Nelson, 1996; Santos, 2005), and they undoubtedly reshaped the institutional landscape in regard to policing and gender (Carrington, Guala, Puyol, & Sozzo, 2020). In order to staff them, the police recruited more women, initiating a shift in institutional culture. As these female officers rose up the ranks, they often led on further initiatives to tackle domestic violence and feminicide, as Chapter Three will demonstrate. The DEAMs offered victims of gender-based violence access to justice and, in the large metropolitan areas where they operate, they have acted as a catalyst for the formation of local victim-support networks. They also play a key role in feminicide prevention as they enforce the protection orders brought in by the 2006 law on domestic violence. This law, which gave the DEAMs and other law enforcement actors much more comprehensive and specific powers to protect and assist victims, then gave another major impetus to the judicial system to develop new structures, practices, and procedures, analysed mainly by Brazilian researchers. Yet, police innovations in response to this and the 2015 feminicide law have not attracted the attention they merit. This book updates the literature on how Brazil's police and justice agencies have reacted to social pressure to improve their responses to violence against women.

GENESIS, METHODOLOGY, AND SOURCES

Since the early 1990s, I have been researching how women's movements in Latin America influence the policymaking process, especially in relation to violence against women, through strategic engagement with political parties and legislative arenas, state bureaucracies, and local as well as national levels of government. My work at Amnesty International as its Brazil researcher in the late 1990s immersed me in the dynamics of that country's criminal justice system and alerted me to the importance of understanding how reform attempts succeed, not just how they fail. It gave me the opportunity to talk to many law enforcement professionals across the country, and to observe the complex, and bumpy, processes by which new policies and approaches to violence reduction were developed by local researchers, academics, policymakers, and criminal justice-sector professionals, and how these related to the absence, or presence, of national reform initiatives.

One national thinktank, the Brazilian Forum on Public Safety (*Fórum Brasileiro de Segurança Pública* – FBSP), has provided a unique space for these communities of practice to work together, produce data, and analyse their own policy experiences around reducing crime, violence, and insecurity. It has prioritised research into gender-based violence and runs an annual competition to recognise good policy and practice in this area. For several years I have worked with the FBSP to develop materials for training law enforcement personnel (FBSP, 2020b). Piloting these materials across the country gave me further opportunity to learn about local initiatives for combatting domestic violence and feminicide from the police and justice professionals we were training.

Encouraging these professionals to recount their triumphs and challenges was consciously rooted in the methodological principles of appreciative enquiry, an approach that focusses on institutional strengths and capacities, rather than on weaknesses. Appreciative enquiry has been adopted from the area of management studies into many different policy fields, yet relatively little into criminal justice studies. This approach forms part of the book's mixed methods which combine process tracing with qualitative case study analysis. The book draws on those conversations with law enforcement officials and reformers, as well as on databases created by civil society organisations and government data and documents. It also foregrounds knowledge produced by law enforcement officials themselves. This unpublished 'pracademic' research conducted fuses academic methods with professional practice-based observation and has, in many cases, informed policy changes. By appreciating what *has* been achieved, even if many challenges and institutional deficits remain, this book demonstrates that sticky problems like feminicide *can* be tackled with enough social pressure, political will, and institutional responsiveness.

The rest of this chapter sets out how and why feminicide emerged as a concept and came to be regarded as a serious global issue affecting women's human security, why it is particularly associated with Latin America, how international and regional norms developed in relation to gender-based violence, and how criminal justice systems are being asked to respond to it. It also sets the scene for understanding how Brazil began to tackle feminicide.

FEMINICIDE: THE EMERGENCE OF A CONCEPT

Murder is not just murder. All acts of violence have a social context and hold a set of meanings for the perpetrator, the victims, and those who observe the violence. The intentional killing of another human being can occur for a multitude of motivations. The degree of societal disapproval, or approval, of the killing hinges on a number of variables – who is killed, by whom, and for what reason. These variables underpin the classifications in law of different forms of lethal violence such as self-defence, manslaughter, homicide, infanticide, and honour killings.

Activist and feminist Diana Russell was instrumental in bringing into usage the term femicide to mean not the homicide of women in general terms but rather 'the misogynous killing of women by men' (Radford & Russell, 1992, p. 3).[8] The targeted mass killing of 14 women, mainly female engineering students, at the University of Montréal in December 1989 by a man who made explicit his hatred and resentment towards women *in general* (he did not personally know the victims) opened up global debate about how women could be the victims of a category-based hate crime analogous to those motivated by racial or religious intolerance. In 1991, the White Ribbon campaign, a movement of men pledging their active opposition to violence against women, was founded in Canada (Kaufman, 2001), whilst a conference at Rutgers University kicked off the '16 Days of Activism against Gender-based Violence' campaign that has been taken up around the globe and is now an annual event every November (Roche, Biron, & Reilly, 1995).

The 1990s also saw a new focus for concern emerge around the extraordinary number of murders of women in Ciudad Juárez, in the northern border Mexican state of Chihuahua. Between 1993 and 2003, at least 370 young women were murdered by persons apparently unknown (Amnesty International, 2003). Around one-third of them had been brutally sexually assaulted, often following abduction, and their bodies dumped on the roadside, in vacant lots, or in the countryside.[9] The majority of victims were young, working class, mixed race women, and many employed by the local assembly factories (*maquiladoras*). From 2000 onwards, the phenomenon began to be recognised in the neighbouring countries of Central America, where exceptionally high levels of lethal violence against women were driven by weak rule of law, poverty, gangs, and violent masculinities created by that region's preceding civil wars (Fregoso & Bejarano, 2010).

Mexican academic, activist, and politician Marcela Lagarde y de los Rios found in Radford and Russell's (1992) work a useful concept for what was happening in Chihuahua and opted to translate 'femicide' as *feminicidio*. She felt that *femicidio* would be understood simply as female homicide, that is, the murder of a woman for any reason, and that this would fail to indicate the misogynistic motivations behind many killings (Lagarde, 2006). She also intended *feminicidio* to denote a situation where such murders were effectively condoned and encouraged by state indifference and inaction. However,

Russell found this usage problematic because, if the state *does* investigate and punish a killing, is it then disqualified as a feminicide? The question of state accountability and responsibility to change the culture and practices of the criminal justice system in order to tackle lethal hate crime against women lies at the heart of this book.[10]

The term *feminicidio* became subsequently popularised around Latin America as women's networks in the region took up the issue, but without the supposed conceptual distinctions between the two possible terms.[11] This is further complicated by the issue of translation from English. In both Spanish and Portuguese, the word *femenina/feminina* means 'female'. It may also connote 'feminine', a marker term for the various ways that society expects women to behave and present themselves. Thus, the 2015 Brazilian definition of *feminicídio* refers to women being murdered based on their *condição de sexo feminino,* essentially a translation of Diana Russell's later definition of the killing of females by males *because they are females.* In this book, I use the term feminicide to echo the terminology used in Brazil.

As the debate about feminicide and impunity was taken up around the region and by international bodies within the UN and the inter-American system, the understanding of feminicide became more sophisticated. Lethal gender-based violence can take many forms. It can be direct, inter-personal violence (a murder), or it can result indirectly from deep-rooted structures of discrimination against women and girls. Many different kinds of gender-based violence could be classified as feminicide using Russell's definition. Direct and intentional forms of feminicide include dowry-related killings of women in South Asia, female infanticide and foeticide in China and Central and South Asia, killings of women accused of sorcery or witchcraft, 'honour-based' killings, stoning to death of women for adultery under extremist interpretations of Sharia law, the murder of women trafficked into forced prostitution, and the targeting of women, often of specific ethnic and/or religious groups, in the context of armed and genocidal conflict. More indirect forms of violence encompass the deaths of women and girls due to denial of bodily autonomy, in the cases of female genital mutilation and infection with HIV by sexual partners who refuse to use protection. Women also die due to denial of healthcare and lack of access to contraception and safe termination of pregnancy. However, for reasons of space and scope this book restricts its analysis to direct and intentional feminicide. It examines mainly domestic-related violence, which accounts for most killings of women and girls, as well as the smaller number of misogynistic killings committed by strangers, neighbours, or acquaintances, which includes lesbo- and transphobic feminicides.

THIRTY YEARS OF GLOBAL ACTIVISM AND POLICY DEVELOPMENT

As the new wave of the women's movement emerged in the 1970s, gender-based violence became a key pre-occupation. Through the 1970s and 1980s, feminists set up shelters to house women fleeing domestic violence, and Reclaim the Night marches highlighted women's fear of sexual violence, assault, and murder outside the home.[12] Governments responded slowly to the movement's demands, largely by putting in place further social safety nets for victims, and did not address prevention or improved criminal justice responses. It was not until the 1990s that violence against women was placed at the centre of international debates on human rights, women's rights and development.

The 1979 UN Convention for the Elimination of all Forms of Discrimination Against Women (CEDAW) laid important groundwork for later shifts in state policy and practice (Šimonović, 2014). However, it contained no explicit reference to violence against women and focussed chiefly on discrimination around employment and civil, political, and economic rights. Its statements on inter-personal relations, family structures, practices, and customs were generic in nature. It had been drafted at a time when abuse of women in the private sphere was seen as an agenda item pushed by Western feminists, a colonialist interference in tradition and custom, and an irrelevance to the 'real' priorities of women in developing countries: poverty and lack of access to basic services (Freeman, Chinkin, & Rudolf, 2012). Nonetheless, the Convention's concern with eliminating de facto as well as de jure discrimination and inequality led to the inclusion of some important enabling language that would oblige States Parties to take specific action to protect women from violence. Article 4.1 urged governments to adopt 'temporary special measures' that would not be considered discrimination as long as their objectives were the attainment of 'equality of opportunity and treatment' between men and women. Article 5.1(a) further advocated 'all appropriate measures' to

> modify the social and cultural patterns of conduct of men and women, with a view to achieving the elimination of prejudices and customary and all other practices which are based on the idea of the inferiority or the superiority of either of the sexes or on stereotyped roles for men and women.

Countries such as Brazil that have brought in laws and policies addressing violence specifically against women are thus complying with international human rights law.

Through the 1980s, the women's movement lobbied the UN agencies dedicated to crime prevention and criminal justice. The watershed year was 1985, when the UN Committee on Crime Prevention and Control put violence against women on the agenda of its Seventh Congress. The UN General Assembly adopted its first resolution on domestic violence and called on the Secretary General to commission more research on the topic from a criminological perspective. The Nairobi Forward-Looking Strategies for the Advancement of Women, adopted at the World Conference that year, also broke new ground in referring to 'gender-specific violence' under 'Abused Women' (UN, 1986, para. 288). Governments were urged to 'establish or strengthen' assistance to victims of violence in the family and society, increase public awareness, suppress degrading representations of women, re-educate offenders, and institute public policies and legislation to eradicate the problem. Nevertheless, these broad recommendations constituted little more than a footnote in an 88-page document still focussed on traditional development concerns (Macaulay, 2000a).

Violence against women was initially framed as a health and social welfare issue and a criminal justice concern. But the policy responses from these two sectors were largely weak, ineffective, and disconnected from one another. The issue shifted, finally, into the human rights field with the UN World Conference on Human Rights held in June 1993 (Bunch & Frost, 2000). The Vienna Declaration and Programme of Action affirmed explicitly that women's rights are an 'unalienable, integral, and indivisible' component of universal human rights, not discretionary or optional. It also moved gender concerns from the field of development, where policy recommendations are non-binding, into that of binding international standards, where UN monitoring mechanisms carry more clout with governments. Women's rights were one of the few areas in the Declaration on which there were concrete recommendations, and the innovations in the text were in large part the result of groundwork done by the CEDAW treaty body.

In particular its General Recommendation 19, adopted in 1992, informed subsequent international norm development with its definition of 'violence that is directed against a woman because she is a woman, or that affects women disproportionately' (CEDAW, 1992). This language foreshadows both Russell's later formulation of femicide and the wording of Brazil's 2015 feminicide law. The Recommendation also established violence against women as a form of sex-based discrimination, prohibited in Article 1 of CEDAW, thus placing an international legal obligation on States Parties to prevent, investigate, and punish all such acts and provide reparation. Further, it required them to exercise 'due diligence' in combatting gender-based violence in public and private life, thereby identifying for the first time the problem of state negligence, as opposed to direct responsibility, where the state may tolerate rather than perpetrate violence. Moreover, it made states accountable for unchecked abuse of women in the private sphere.

Six months after the Vienna Conference, the UN General Assembly adopted an even more comprehensive statement. The Declaration on the Elimination of Violence Against Women defined three distinct loci of violence against women: in the family and home, in the community, and at the hands of agents of the state.[13] It also explicitly rejected cultural relativist arguments by prohibiting states from invoking custom, tradition, or religion as justification for abdicating their responsibility to condemn and eradicate violence against women. It noted that violence was 'a manifestation of historically unequal power relations' and 'domination' of men over women, and that violence was a crucial social mechanism of subordination. The Declaration reiterated General Recommendation 19's emphasis on the expected 'due diligence' of states, which continues to inform the work of monitoring mechanisms. The Declaration additionally required states to allocate budget, develop national action plans, and train law enforcement officials on gender-based violence. It urged states to collect and report data, report to the UN mechanisms, and support local women's groups and NGOs. These broader requirements have been echoed in feminist movement demands in Latin America because these kinds of practices turn paper declarations into effective protections.

CEDAW's Optional Protocol, which came into force in 2000, is a key mechanism for holding states to account. It allows the CEDAW Committee to hear complaints by individuals, and to investigate grave and systematic violations of women's rights, which it did in the case of the mass disappearances of women and sexually motivated feminicides in Ciudad Juárez (UN, 2005). Another important enforcement mechanism is the UN Special Rapporteur (UNSR) on Violence against Women. The post was set up in 1994 after the Vienna Conference to conduct field visits to countries and report to the UN Human Rights Council (previously the Commission on Human Rights). Much of the UNSR's mandate has focussed on feminicide, even before that concept was widely accepted. Killings of women are examined systematically during country visits and in 1999 the UNSR presented a thematic report on violence in the family to the Commission, noting that conservative gender ideologies that restricted women's roles to being wives and mothers exposed women who did not conform to traditional sex roles to gender-based hate crimes. In her view, such ideologies legitimated honour killings and other forms of feminicide (UN, 1999). This was followed by a further thematic report, in 2002, on cultural practices within the family that inflicted violence on women, such as honour killings carried out by husbands, fathers, brothers, or uncles, sometimes on behalf of tribal councils (UN, 2002).

In 2011, the UNSR organised an international expert meeting on the gender-motivated killing of women in order to build on existing expertise in relation to the expressions and underlying causes of feminicide. The UNSR's 2012 report to the Human Rights Council focussed on the different types of feminicide, whilst the 2016 report called for the establishment of feminicide watches (UN, 2012, 2016). This was also the start of looking critically at state responses, identifying regional good practices and lessons learned, and discussing policy, legal, and institutional challenges at the national, regional, and international levels. In the Conclusions of its 57th Session, the Commission on the Status of Women urged states to

> *Strengthen national legislation, where appropriate, to punish violent gender-related killings of women and girls, and integrate specific mechanisms or policies to prevent, investigate and eradicate such deplorable forms of gender-based violence. (UN, 2013, para. 34e)*

A month later, in April 2013, the Commission on Crime Prevention and Criminal Justice considered a statement submitted by the Academic Council on the UN System that became known as the Vienna Declaration on Femicide (ECOSOC, 2013).[14] The conceptual gap between women's rights and crime and security policy began narrowing as criminal justice agencies increasingly understood that tackling violence in the home was not optional or secondary but rather a core task of law enforcement.

PUTTING GENDER-BASED VIOLENCE ON THE AGENDA IN LATIN AMERICA

As a region, Latin America has been at the forefront of the feminicide debate, in part due to geographical concentrations of a specific sort of sexual murder. However, its leadership on this is also the result of the early emergence of its regional human rights system and pioneering and comprehensive hard law on gender-based violence that addressed not just access to justice, but also protection and prevention. Both factors produced ground-breaking jurisprudence that pushed states in the region to act.

The decade following the 1979 adoption of CEDAW saw the transition from authoritarian to democratic rule in several countries in Latin America. The newly elected democratic governments were keen to prove themselves committed players in the international field and demonstrate their support for the social issues over which their military predecessors had been so harshly criticised. They also wanted to attract electoral support from women, conscious of their leading role in the pro-democracy movements. Brazil, Chile, Argentina, and other countries quickly signed up to international human rights instruments as a means of locking themselves into a global system of democratic standards. Women's organisations saw an opportunity to extend gender equality and, spurred by the Nairobi and Beijing conference processes, they built networks and mobilised on three planes, nationally, regionally, and internationally.

The advance in global norms and the pressure from feminist groups led Latin America to become the first region in the world to produce legally binding international law regarding violence against women, in the Organization of American States' (OAS) Belém do Pará Convention. Two inter-American women's mechanisms were critical in establishing the regional norms contained in the Convention, and in promoting their national adoption and implementation (Friedman, 2009). The first is the Inter-American Commission of Women (*Comisión Interamericana de Mujeres* – CIM), set up in 1928 to promote women's rights in the region. This it did by developing new legal norms and international commitments with which OAS member states were then obliged to align their national legislation. In 1988, CIM noted that violence against women was absent in CEDAW and in the laws of the region, and in 1990 began a wide-ranging consultation process (Poole, 2013).[15] It convened two meetings of experts to draft a new regional convention, bringing together an effective epistemic community of legal experts, diplomats, criminal justice operators, legislators, educators, sociologists, and psychologists (Meyer, 1999, p. 67). The final version was adopted on 9 June 1994 at the 24th ordinary General Assembly of the OAS held in the Brazilian city of Belém do Pará.

The Inter-American Convention surpasses the UN Declaration in its provisions. The site of domestic violence is defined much more widely to encompass any arrangement or inter-personal relationship in which the aggressor may have shared a home with the victim. Many of the recommendations resemble those of the Declaration, but emphasise legal reform and access to simple, rapid recourse through the courts, urging states to set up fair and efficient legal procedures that offer women effective protection. The Convention, in conjunction with mobilisation by women's organisations around the 1995 UN Conference on Women, held in Beijing, prompted most countries across the region to pass new legislation on domestic violence through the latter part of the 1990s.[16] Also, unlike CEDAW, the Convention provides an individual right of petition and allows NGOs to lodge complaints with the Inter-American Commission on Human Rights (IACHR) if the State Party fails in its obligations. This was to prove critical to Brazilian feminist groups that helped Maria da Penha, whose husband had never been punished for attempted feminicide, take her case to the Commission in 1998. The ensuing judgement, criticising the Brazilian government for its lack of due diligence, created a new precedent in inter-American jurisprudence (IACHR, 2001) and helped Brazil finally pass a law on domestic violence.

Nonetheless, enforcement and application of the new anti-domestic violence laws and of the various commitments laid out in the Convention proved a challenge. In 1994, the IACHR had also created the position of Special Rapporteur on the Rights of Women with a mandate similar to the UNSR to conduct field visits to States Parties and make recommendations. However, its reports proved insufficient to prompt significant action. So, a decade later, the inter-American system launched a second monitoring body, the Follow-up Mechanism to the Belém do Pará Convention (known by its Spanish acronym *Mecanismo de Seguimiento de la Convención de Belém do Pará* – MESECVI). This is a permanent multi-lateral evaluation instrument that operates on the basis of exchange and technical co-operation between the States Parties and a Committee of Experts, set up in 2005. With a remit to analyse progress in implementation and find ways round the most entrenched obstacles, in 2014 it launched a guide to applying the convention (MESECVI, 2014). Notable progress on gender-based violence has been achieved in three phases by the inter-American system through the CIM, the MESECVI, and their collaboration with women's movement advocates. First, the hard law was created, then these actors operated a 'pincer' strategy on national governments, getting them to adopt the regional norms through national legislation by moving back and forth between refining regional strategies and encouraging national-level implementation (Friedman, 2009, p. 359).

THE POLITICAL ENVIRONMENT OF RESPONSES TO GENDER-BASED VIOLENCE IN BRAZIL

Brazil offers something of a paradox in relation to women's rights policy. At the international and regional levels, it was, until very recently, an enthusiastic norm entrepreneur supporting gender equality in forums such as the CIM and the Vienna and Beijing conferences. But when it came to implementing, and reporting back on, its adherence to those international standards, the national government was often reluctant and non-compliant (Roggeband, 2016).[17] Brazil's first official report on CEDAW was submitted 17 years late, in 2002, and only under women's movement pressure.[18] It was slow in passing national legislation and developing national-level policy on gender-based violence: it was the last country in the region to enact its first domestic violence law, and defined feminicide as a crime only after 16 others had done so. This contrasts with the success of women's movement engagement with sub-national governments, which have instituted notable practical policy innovations such as the DEAMs and the domestic violence police patrols analysed in Chapter Five. Feminist groups also resorted to using supra-national bodies to put pressure on national government actors in a classic 'boomerang' move (Keck & Sikkink, 1998).

Domestic and sexual violence were highlighted as problems in Brazil by the women's movement in the 1970s in response to a number of high-profile acquittals of men who had committed feminicide. Women's groups played an important role in the process of re-democratisation, and demands for civil and political rights intertwined. By the late 1970s, Brazil's civil–military regime, which lasted from 1964 to 1985, was thawing politically. This enabled the 'official' opposition party, the Brazilian Democratic Movement Party (*Partido do Movimento Democrático Brasileiro* – PMDB) to elect state governors and mayors, giving female party activists leverage to demand new institutions to promote women's equality (Alvarez, 1990). In 1983, the PMDB-led state government in São Paulo established the first governmental mechanism for women's rights (*Conselho Estadual da Condição Feminina*) and in 1985 inaugurated Latin America's first DEAM.

When the new civilian government took power in 1985, it set up a federal-level mechanism, the National Council for Women's Rights (*Conselho Nacional dos Direitos da Mulher* – CNDM), as an advisory body attached to the Ministry of Justice. Staffed by feminists, the CNDM was key in galvanising women around the drafting of the new constitution. Their nation-wide consultation resulted in a national women's charter containing demands that the 26 women elected to the Constitutional Assembly were able to incorporate, in very large part, into the constitution approved in 1988 (Pitanguy, 2018). It provides that,

> The State shall guarantee assistance to the family, as represented
> by each one of the persons that makes up that family, by creating
> mechanisms to deter violence in the framework of the relationships
> among those family members.[19]

However, despite this new onus on the state, further government action to tackle violence against women proved slow in the 1990s. At the instigation of a number of feminist federal deputies, Brazil's Chamber of Deputies ran a Parliamentary Committee of Inquiry into gender-based violence from January 1991 to August 1992, but with modest outcomes (Câmara dos Deputados, 1993). Even though the Belém do Pará Convention was launched on Brazilian territory in 1994, it failed to prompt the government to pass a law on domestic violence. Weldon (2002) argues that the likelihood of governments acting decisively against domestic violence is a function, not of the absolute or relative strength of the women's movement locally, but rather of its influence on the state, and in Brazil this was relatively weak by the mid-1990s. This was exacerbated by the movement's lack of consensus on legal strategies and its public policy focus on providing specialist legal and social services to victims, such as shelters and police stations (Macaulay, 2000a, 2000b, p. 361; Senado Federal, 2013). When other countries were formulating their national legislation on domestic violence, Brazil launched a new judicial forum, designed without public consultation or women's movement input, that ended up handling non-lethal domestic violence cases (Macaulay, 2005, p. 218). The new criminal misdemeanour courts (*Juizados Especiais Criminais* – JECrims) introduced in 1995 were inappropriate for such a task because they effectively downplayed the seriousness of domestic violence and stressed inter-personal mediation over protection for the victim. Although they distracted attention in the short term away from the need for specific legislation, in the medium term, disquiet about these courts motivated feminist jurists to draw up an alternative to the JECrims.

Actors in the international system also became concerned at Brazil's continuing failure to develop comprehensive and joined-up policies to protect women effectively. The UNSR chose Brazil for her first full country study on violence against women in July 1996 precisely due to the gap she identified between the 'many existing programmes and activities, both governmental and non-governmental, to combat and prevent such violence' and the 'high prevalence of such violence in the country' (ECOSOC, 1997, p. 2). In her report, she noted 'the general failure of the Brazilian criminal justice system to investigate and prosecute, in a non-discriminatory manner, crimes of domestic violence against women'.

It was this systemic failure of the criminal justice system that led feminist activists to enlist the regional human rights system to put pressure on the Brazilian government in what would be a landmark case. Maria da Penha had been shot in 1983 by her husband whilst she slept, leaving her paraplegic. He later tried to electrocute her as she was recovering. He was charged with attempted murder but 15 years later was still free, his conviction not yet finalised. In 1998, assisted by two human rights NGOs, Center for Justice and International Law and the Latin American and Caribbean Committee for the Defence of Women's Rights, Maria da Penha took her case to the IACHR. She alleged that failure to convict and sentence her violent husband constituted a violation of the various human rights conventions to which Brazil is a State Party, including CEDAW, the Belém do Pará Convention, and the American Convention on Human Rights. The Brazilian government failed to respond to any of the communications sent by the IACHR, which in 2001 issued a report declaring Brazil to be guilty of negligence, omission, and tolerance of violence against women. This marked a number of firsts in the inter-American human rights system itself: never before had the Commission heard a case related to domestic violence, found a State Party in violation of women's rights for its failure to act, or issued a decision about failure to comply with the Belém do Pará Convention. Despite the Brazil government's apparent indifference to the report, the ruling gave campaigners the leverage they needed to update Brazil's laws, both working within Brazilian governmental, legislative, and legal spaces, and co-ordinating with international organisations. In 2002, revisions to the country's civil code established full equality between men and women and a consortium of feminist NGOs, jurists, and legal experts seized the initiative to start drafting and consulting widely on a new law that would remove domestic violence from the problematic jurisdiction of the JECrims (Campos, 2011; Carone, 2018). The consortium also submitted a shadow report to Brazil's first report to the CEDAW treaty body, highlighting the Maria da Penha case. The CEDAW committee was also clear: Brazil must pass a law on domestic violence without delay (CEDAW, 2003, para. 113).

The timing was good: women's movement influence on national government had increased greatly with the 2002 election of President Luiz Inácio Lula da Silva of the Workers' Party (*Partido dos Trabalhadores* – PT). This was a much more conducive political environment as the PT had been supported by women's groups from its foundation, and backed many feminist policies (Macaulay, 2006). During nearly 14 years of PT government (2003–2016), Brazil moved from being a state reluctant to comply with its international obligations to one that actively developed policies on gender-based violence. On the first day in government in 2003, the President created the Special Secretariat for Policies for Women (*Secretaria Especial de Políticas para as Mulheres* – SPM). Its Secretary of State had a status equivalent to a minister and a seat in the cabinet, and she reported directly to the President's office. The strengthening of the women's rights machinery in national government provided an executive body that could be an interlocutor with international bodies such as UN Women and their representatives in Brazil, with regional bodies, both inter-governmental and non-governmental, and with the national women's movements and NGOs. It also had the capacity, for the first time, to lead and invest in government-wide policy. In 2004, the government launched the First National Plan of Policies for Women (*Plano Nacional de Políticas para as Mulheres*), based on extensive consultations conducted via municipal, state level, and national conferences. One of the four pillars addressed the best way to tackle violence against women. Dialogue between criminal justice actors, women's groups, and other relevant parties around the country, led by the feminist consortium, the SPM, and an inter-ministerial working group, resulted in the Maria da Penha law on domestic violence being passed unanimously in the National Congress in 2006, which completed the first stage of the campaign. The second cycle of mobilisation focussed on the implementation of the new legal apparatus, through a national monitoring group (*Observatório Nacional de Implementação e Aplicação da Lei Maria da Penha*) set up by women's groups and feminist academics in universities around the country, and funded by the SPM and international development assistance (Maciel, 2011).

Effective application of the law has depended on the support of all three branches of government – executive, legislature, and the judiciary – and at all three levels of government – federal, state, and municipal. Women have built up a strategic presence within both the legislative and executive branches since the late 1980s. Female legislators elected to the National Congress have acted effectively as a cross-party women's caucus (*bancada feminina*) despite their relatively small numbers (never more than 10% until 2019), and violence against women proved a topic around which they could coalesce. The *bancada* worked closely with women's organisations and with the national women's machinery (CNDM and SPM), was crucial to the passage of both the Maria da Penha and feminicide bills, and monitored subsequent implementation of both. It also embedded its formal institutional reach within Congress. The Women's Advocacy Office (*Procuradoria da Mulher*) was set up in 2009 to monitor all government programmes, look into reports of violence against women and discrimination, and co-operate with national and international bodies to promote women's rights. All proposed legislation is now screened for its impact on gender inequalities. In 2013, the Lower House created a Women's Secretariat (*Secretaria da Mulher*), within which sit the *Procuradoria da Mulher* and Co-ordinating Committee on Women's Rights (*Coordenadoria da Mulher*). The latter represents the *bancada feminina* and has a seat in the college of party leaders with the right to speak, vote, and use time on the floor of the house ordinarily allocated only to a party leader.

Brazil is unusual amongst countries with a federal system of government in that its legal codes are unitary and national in scope, but it is the 27 subnational governments (26 states and the Federal District of Brasília) that administer the agencies that apply the country's laws. Each has a law enforcement agency (*Secretaria de Segurança Pública*) that governs both a uniformed military police force, whose role is to patrol the streets and respond to calls, and a smaller civil police force that investigates crime and liaises with the judicial branch (prosecutors and courts).[20] Around 1,000 towns have set up municipal guards charging with maintaining 'social peace'. The justice agencies (courts, prosecutor's, and public defender's offices) are similarly devolved.

Therefore, the coalition of legislative, executive, and civil society forces created at national level needed to be replicated in similar, horizontal alliances at state and, often, municipal levels. Brazil's strong federalism creates symmetries through the three layers of government, and so the women's rights mechanisms are mirrored in the states and 5,570 municipalities, in both a vertical and horizontal mainstreaming effect (Macaulay, 2010). Many state legislative assemblies and some municipal ones now have a *procuradoria* with a focus on gender-based violence, following a model promoted by the one in Congress. Every state government has both a policymaking body and a consultative *conselho*, with representation of civil society and relevant governmental bodies, to promote gender equality (IBGE, 2019), as do many municipalities.[21]

The existence of these governmental and non-governmental networks at all governance levels has been fundamental to directing sufficient attention and resources to gender-based violence and bringing together diverse public bodies. In 2009, the Lula government created a sub-secretariat within the SPM dedicated to addressing violence against women. This was upgraded to a secretariat in 2012, after the SPM received full ministerial status in 2010. National policy developed quickly through two National Conferences and two Plans of Policies for Women (in 2004 and 2008), both of which prioritised violence against women. Between 2005 and 2006, the federal government signed 168 agreements with municipal and state governments (Senado Federal, 2013, p. 43), and in 2007 a National Pact on Violence against Women (*Pacto Nacional de Enfrentamento à Violência contra as Mulheres*) brought together 10 ministries, co-ordinated by the SPM, with state level and municipal governments and women's organisations. Its revision in 2011 extended the partnership to the judicial agencies, whose responses are examined in Chapter Two. The pact's aims included strengthening the networks of support to victims, improving access to justice, and ensuring that the Maria da Penha law was properly applied. The local women's policy machineries detailed above were fundamental to implementing the pact as they acted as the formal conduits through which SPM could channel funding for federal–local agreements.

The construction and consolidation over the last 15 years of these intra- and inter-institutional architectures have given government bodies capacity to begin dealing better with domestic violence. In 2019, a National Pact for the Prevention of Domestic Violence was signed by the three branches of government, with the National Justice Council (*Conselho Nacional de Justiça –* CNJ) and Federal Supreme Court (*Supremo Tribunal Federal –* STF) representing the judiciary, the Minister of Justice the executive branch, and the *bancada feminina* the national legislature. Local networks of support services have expanded, if very unevenly, across Brazil, ranging from multi-agency victim-support centres, shelters, and sexual violence units, to perpetrator programmes.[22] As the following chapters show, the criminal justice system agencies had developed dedicated services such as women's police stations, domestic violence police patrols, special investigation units, domestic violence courts, and specialist prosecutor and legal aid teams. These policies and institutional machineries were able to develop specific policies around feminicide relatively quickly, even before the passage of the 2015 feminicide law, when it became clear that the other policies dedicated to assisting victims of domestic violence were not making a dent in feminicide statistics.

NEW RIGHT POLITICS AND 'GENDER PHOBIA'

In 2014, another PT president, Dilma Rousseff, took office for her second term and backed the 2015 feminicide bill. However, the receptive political environment for women's policy networks came to an end in 2016 with her controversial impeachment. Her Vice-President, Michel Temer, took over as interim president whilst the country was in turmoil over a huge corruption scandal in the state sector and an economic recession. The SPM was reabsorbed, along with the CNDM, into a restructured justice ministry, completing a process of downgrading minority rights mechanisms that had begun for fiscal reasons at the end of 2015. The political shift to the extreme right was completed in October 2018 when Brazil elected to the presidency Jair Bolsonaro, a long-time legislator who until that point had been notorious chiefly for his intemperate outbursts, crude language, open misogyny, homophobia, and other authoritarian values. It seemed that the Bolsonaro government would preside over a swift dismantling of many of the gains in gender equality and women's rights that had been progressively won since the 1980s. Some of his initial executive actions confirmed this fear as he set up the Ministry of Women, the Family and Human Rights (*Ministério da Mulher, da Família e dos Direitos Humanos*), playing to a Christian base that strongly associates women with family and caring responsibilities. An Evangelical pastor, Damares Alves, prone to somewhat bizarre pronouncements about women's role in society, was appointed as the new minister. During the election campaign, and after his government took office, he, his ministers, and his party's representatives regularly launched attacks on 'gender ideology', which they promised to root out of the educational curriculum (Machado, 2018). 'Gender ideology' is a *bête noire* of the neo-Pentecostals and other right-wing groups and since 2019 Brazil has joined forces internationally with fundamentalist Muslim countries and the Vatican to veto the use of the word 'gender' in UN documents. This places Brazil dramatically at odds with its historical path of being a global good citizen and progressive norm entrepreneur. Yet, the norm- and institution-building work on gender-based violence carried out over the last three decades has made for a resilient and dense network, inside and outside government. The story told in the next four chapters shows that concern about violence against women has been mainstreamed in justice-sector agencies, enabling them to develop some effective and innovative policies to tackle feminicide even in what might seem an unpropitious political environment.

Chapter Two analyses how legislation on gender-based violence has been a key factor in prompting state action. It outlines how the comprehensive law on domestic violence impelled the criminal justice system to build new institutional capacity that underpinned its response to anti-feminicide legislation. It examines the anti-feminicide legislation passed in Latin America and describes the political environment and strategic process that helped Brazil's law to get passed. Chapter Three shows how the new laws and pressure from women's groups for effective implementation has led policy entrepreneurs to begin reforming the police forces' cognitive and bureaucratic routines to better recognise, register, and investigate murders of women. These routines are still challenged when the violence is rooted not just in domestic violence, but also in other factors such as race, transsexual identities, and criminal activity. Chapter Four analyses the role of the judicial institutions, which are becoming more agile in bringing feminicide cases successfully to trial, and whose national leadership has made clear its disapproval of victim-blaming defence arguments. Chapter Five details some of the feminicide prevention strategies developed by the justice system, such as domestic violence police patrols, monitoring perpetrators, risk assessment, addressing gender-based violence within the law enforcement institutions, and training criminal justice staff. It also highlights the importance of community education around gender relations, which faces significant obstacles in a political environment where far right and religious groups are hostile to such discussions. Chapter Six draws out the key original findings of this study and identifies some lessons from the Brazilian case, not just for Latin America but also for the very many other countries attempting to get to grips with this seemingly entrenched problem.

NOTES

1. Searching online with the Portuguese phrase 'Mulher é morta a facadas' for a sample three-month period from January to March 2020, I turned up dozens of cases.

2. www.femicidescensus.org.

3. All translations are my own.

4. This phrase is used repeatedly by the World Health Organization.

5. Its full title is the Council of Europe Convention on Preventing and Combating Violence against Women and Domestic Violence.

6. This protocol resulted from a joint effort of the Office of the United Nations High Commissioner for Human Rights and UN Women, and was strongly supported by the Conference of the States Parties to the Belém do Pará Convention, and the General Assembly of the Ibero-American Association of Prosecutor's Offices.

7. Data on intentional homicides of female victims, by country, is available at https://data.worldbank.org/indicator/VC.IHR.PSRC.FE.P5.

8. She first coined the term femicide in 1976 when testifying at the first International Tribunal on Crimes Against Women in Brussels. https://www.dianarussell.com/origin_of_femicide.html.

9. Estimates of the number of women murdered in the area vary wildly due to very poor criminal justice data and record keeping.

10. For more detail on the debate over the implications of the terms femicide and feminicide see Deus and Gonzalez (2018, pp. 12–22).

11. Diana Russell initially sanctioned the translation of femicide as *feminicidio* but subsequently changed her mind. https://www.dianarussell.com/origin_of_femicide.html.

12. The Reclaim the Night marches started in 1977 in Leeds, England, in response to a wave of murders and attempted murders of women committed over several years by a serial killer known as the Yorkshire Ripper.

13. Adopted on 20 December 1993 in General Assembly Resolution A/48/104. Conventions are legally binding, whereas declarations are not.

14. ACUNS is an NGO with consultative status to the Economic and Social Council Commission on Crime Prevention and Criminal Justice.

15. This was preceded by an Inter-American Consultation on Women and Violence in 1990, and the Declaration on the Eradication of Violence against Women adopted by the 25th Assembly of Delegates of the Inter-American Commission of Women.

16. For a list of the 'first generation' laws on domestic violence, see Friedman (2009, p. 350).

17. This was part of a pattern, rather than a specific neglect of women's rights: Brazil's first report to the Committee on Torture was 10 years late when submitted in 2001 and it reported on the International Covenant on Economic,

Social and Cultural Rights only after human rights groups had first submitted a 'shadow' report.

18. The 2002 submission substituted for the five periodic reports that Brazil should have submitted in this time period.

19. Article 226 (para. 8).

20. Brazil has approximately 500,000 serving military police officers, and 100,000 civil police officers. The fire brigade is the other first response institution, under the aegis of the military police.

21. The name of the local government policy bodies for women's right varies, as do their institutional locations.

22. The exact numbers of each vary, as different government bodies publish divergent statistics.

Chapter Two

LEGISLATING FEMINICIDE

INTRODUCTION

The rapidity with which the feminicide law was passed in Brazil in 2015, and criminal justice agencies began to institute specific policies and procedures, owes a great deal to the impact of the Maria da Penha law. This completely changed the legal and institutional landscape for the handling of domestic violence. Chapter One outlined the international and national political contexts in which the law was passed. This one begins by examining the law's innovations and how they prompted transformations within the criminal justice system, specifically within the judicial sector – the courts, the prosecutor's office, and the public defender's (legal aid) office – that primed them to respond to the 2015 feminicide law. Although the criminal justice system is operationally highly decentralised, some national agencies and actors played key roles either as veto players or as policy diffusers. The chapter then looks at the different ways in which Latin American countries approached incorporating feminicide into their criminal codes, before tracing the politics and impact of that process in Brazil.

LEGAL CHANGE IN BRAZIL: FROM DOMESTIC VIOLENCE TO FEMINICIDE

The Maria da Penha law, inspired by the Belém do Pará Convention and by existing good practices around the region, is both comprehensive and innovative in Brazilian terms (Bandeira, 2009; Bandeira & Almeida, 2015). It widens the definition of what constitutes abuse, specifying that it may be physical, psychological, sexual, financial, or reputational. Although it does not use the term 'coercive control', the law is clearly rooted in this understanding of abuse as stemming from power imbalances entrenched not just within the family but also in social structures. The law sets out detailed recommendations on three inter-linked aspects: protection, prevention, and punishment, and thus simultaneously expands both the penal and non-penal dispositions available to the justice system to assist victims and change the behaviour of perpetrators.

In particular, it introduced changes to the court system. Until 1995, any woman reporting abuse to a police station would have their complaint logged either as a crime identifiable in the criminal code (such as bodily harm) or as a non-criminal 'dispute'. Police often dismissed the complaints, seeing them as trivial, or else acted as informal mediators with the aim of reconciling the couple. Only the most serious cases ever reached the courts. This changed between 1995 and 2006 after Law 9.099 created the JECrims, designed to process offences that would otherwise be punishable by up to four years in prison such as minor assault or criminal damage. Like many such courts in Latin America oriented towards alternative dispute resolution, they filled up immediately with cases concerning non-lethal domestic violence cases, for which they had not been designed (Macaulay, 2005), and for which their operating principles and procedures of speed, informality, self-representation, oral argumentation, and direct plaintiff/defendant interaction with the judge or lay mediator were inappropriate (Campos, 2003; Campos & Carvalho, 2006). Cases could be suspended at the discretion of the judge, and the sanctions applied were unsuitable, often a fine of a food parcel. Some 90% of cases ended at the first stage of conciliation, either because the woman was intimidated by the presence of her abuser in court, or because the judge had pressed both sides to settle in order to close the case (Campos, 2003). This approach effectively decriminalised domestic violence and resulted in women being obliged to remain in the home with their abuser, increasing the risk of feminicide.

The alternative law drafted by the feminist legal consortium put forward two key proposals: that domestic violence cases be removed completely from the jurisdiction of the JECrims, and that special domestic violence courts (*Juizados/Varas de Violência Doméstica e Familiar contra a Mulher*) be created to deal with not just the criminal but also the civil aspects of a case, such as divorce and child maintenance arrangements. Predictably, the judiciary was very resistant to institutional change imposed by other actors, and the federation of JECrim judges (*Fórum Nacional dos Juizados Especiais* – FONAJE) tried to veto the removal of domestic violence cases, which constituted the bulk of their work (Lavigne, 2011). Apart from self-interest, this revealed a fundamental disagreement about the nature of domestic violence. For the feminist legal reformers, it constituted a violation of human rights, based on its multi-faceted, prolonged, and cumulative character. However, the criminal code in a civil law system such as Brazil's tends to have a fragmenting effect:

each assault or complaint is evaluated as a discrete event. That would classify a slap in the face or a verbal threat as a misdemeanour – the understanding of the FONAJE judges – rather than as a precursor to more serious harm or as part of a wider pattern of abuse. Brazil needed a law that defined domestic violence in a way that reflected its reality and a judicial arena staffed with trained specialists capable of handling its complexities.

Legal challenges continued after the law was passed. The Attorney General's Office, assisted by the feminist NGO consortium, persuaded the STF to uphold its constitutionality, which it did in several pieces of jurisprudence. Its ruling that the law's focus on women was not discriminatory, on the grounds that compensatory legislation is permissible if it promotes material equality, dealt with a potential objection to the later feminicide law. It also ruled that the removal of domestic violence from the JECrims was legal as it enabled the serious criminal nature of the abuse to be recognised, and that plea bargaining, alternative sentencing and alleging the 'insignificance' of an abusive act was not allowed. Furthermore, it allowed the criminal courts of first instance jurisdiction over both civil and criminal matters in domestic violence cases where no specialised courts existed, and that the law's requirement of the latter did not violate states' autonomy over the court system.[1] In relation to the prosecutor's office, it ruled that arrest, investigation, and prosecution should be automatic (*ação penal pública incondicionada*) in cases of even minor bodily harm, removing the onus from the victim to press charges. The seriousness of domestic violence was repeatedly emphasised and its definition extended, for example, to instances where the victim and perpetrator do not co-habit. This jurisprudence related to the Maria da Penha law was crucial to the feminicide law and its operational definition of domestic abuse.

However, the specialised courts, which had to be created and funded by the state-level judiciaries, were slow to get going, with only six set up in 2006. The CNJ, instituted in 2004 as an oversight body for the country's judiciary, then stepped forward to be the most important driver of nation-wide change in how the country's courts and judges dealt with domestic violence cases. In 2007, it issued a formal recommendation to all the state appellate courts to accelerate the installation of the new courts,[2] and by mid-2020 every single state had at least one, with 139 across the country.[3] These operate with a multi-disciplinary team providing psychological, legal, and welfare support to victims. As they became consolidated, their judges formed a national forum in 2009, which has issued over 50 statements (*enunciados*) about best practice in the application of the law. Whilst not jurisprudential, these further clarify the state's responsibilities in tackling domestic abuse. As will be seen in Chapter Five, these courts are responsible for issuing the emergency protective measures that are key to feminicide prevention.

In 2011, the CNJ, a centralised, top-down body, was able to further build the capacity of the judiciary nation-wide by ordering every state appellate court (*Tribunal de Justiça* – TJ) to create a Committee on Women and Domestic Violence (*Coordenadoria Estadual das Mulheres em Situação de Violência Doméstica e Familiar* – CEVID).[4] The CEVIDs have a remit to improve judicial infrastructure, assist in training magistrates and staff, set up the domestic violence courts, collect relevant data, deal with complaints, and correct failings in the system. Although the level of activity varies from state to state, the CEVIDs have been critical local actors in establishing the multi-agency victim-support networks mandated by the Maria da Penha law, multiplying policies such as the police domestic violence patrols detailed in Chapter Five, replicating good practice from elsewhere in the country, and producing reliable statistics demonstrating progress and areas for improvement. From 2007, the CNJ organised Maria da Penha events and conferences, and from 2015, led by one of the first women supreme justices, Carmen Lúcia Antunes Rocha, the STF, and the CNJ undertook concerted periodic action to clear backlogs of domestic violence cases in the courts.[5] In 2017, the CNJ launched its own National Judiciary Policy for Combatting Violence Against Women (*Política Judiciária Nacional de Enfrentamento à Violência contra as Mulheres*).[6]

The National Council of the Prosecutor's office (*Conselho Nacional do Ministério Público* – CNMP), also established in 2004, took up the cause as well. However, as prosecutors pride themselves on their operational and professional autonomy, the process has been more uneven and less homogeneous. At the top of the pyramid, the National Council of State Attorneys General has a permanent committee on domestic violence. In addition, most state attorney general's offices (*procuradorias*) have a women's rights unit in the capital (they bear a variety of names), and some have regional offices too. In São Paulo state, for example, the Special Task Force on Domestic Violence (*Grupo de Atuação Especial de Enfrentamento à Violência Doméstica* – GEVID) has seven outposts across the state. Article 28 of the Maria da Penha law also requires women victims of domestic violence to have access to free legal aid at all stages, and so the office of the public defender (*Defensoria Pública*), a counterpart in theory to the prosecutor's office but historically something of a poor relation, has also built up its capacity and expertise. Despite being listed in the 1988 Constitution as a key judicial function, not all states had a public defender's office until 2012, and it was only in 2004 that a constitutional amendment guaranteed their 'administrative and functional autonomy' putting them, in principle, on a par with the courts and prosecutor's office. It is also notable for being the most gender-equal judicial service in Brazil, as women constitute half of its over 6,000 lawyers. Each state *defensoria pública* set up women's rights units, all known by the acronym of NUDEM.[7] Some states have just one centralised unit, whilst others have decentralised the service, with several across the state covering a specific geographical area. The development of this judicial capacity meant that Brazil's feminicide law could be more effectively applied than many of the others in the region that pre-dated it.

LATIN AMERICAN LAWS ON FEMINICIDE

The Maria da Penha law named and defined domestic violence as a specific offence with identifiable features because the existing crimes listed in the penal code did not adequately capture the dimensions of abuse and its impact on women and their families. Similar reasons lie behind the anti-feminicide laws passed in Latin America. Feminists have long understood the act of *naming* to be a highly political act, for it makes visible what is ignored, denaturalises what is taken for granted, and displaces competing concepts. Giving gender-based violence a *nomen juris* forces the justice system to engage with new concepts, redefines the legal subject, and reframes fundamental questions of motivation and culpability (Frazer & Hutchings, 2019). The feminist criminology and legal studies that emerged in the 1980s demonstrated how law is not gender neutral, how it imagines women as 'sexed subjects', and how sexual differences are framed, created, and reproduced in social, legal, and criminological discourses. Women's full personhood has been historically diminished in law, either formally through the explicit denial of equal rights, or informally through the interpretation of law. For example, married women in Brazil lacked full capacity until 1962. Up until 2005, the Brazilian criminal code named rape as a 'crime against morals' that could be expunged if the victim married the rapist (a common provision in Latin American laws) and referred to the categories of 'honest woman' and 'virgin'. The revised definition of rape as a 'crime against sexual dignity' gave women legal personhood and bodily autonomy. Sexual harassment (*importunação sexual*) was named as an offence for the first time in 2018. Through reliance on both the language of the law and social norms, the murder of women has been 'discounted' by defence lawyers in court in many socially recognised ways, as a 'domestic' dispute, a crime of love, passion, madness, and impulse, for which the victim is somehow responsible. The feminicide laws passed since 2007 in Latin America were intended to end the patriarchal assumption that women's bodies are possessable and disposable by men (Ávila, 2018; Segato, 2010). These new laws and revisions of old laws have made women 'speakable subjects' (Lacey, 1998), and women's movement mobilisation has been able to shape *how* they are spoken of in law.

The Cotton Field Judgement

It was clear to the regional mechanisms monitoring progress on violence against women that its lethal forms were not adequately defined in law and therefore not handled appropriately by the criminal justice system. By the mid-2000s, the number of women murdered in Mexico and the Northern Triangle of Honduras, Guatemala, and El Salvador was running into the thousands. MESECVI (2008) issued a Declaration that put feminicide firmly on the regional agenda, and Recommendation Six of its Second Hemispheric Report urged states to 'Adopt measures to prevent and punish femicide, in both public and private spheres' (MESECVI, 2012, p. 97). The UN Commission on the Status of Women similarly exhorted states to

> *Strengthen national legislation, where appropriate, to punish violent gender-related killings of women and girls, and integrate specific mechanisms or policies to prevent, investigate and eradicate such deplorable forms of gender-based violence. (UN, 2013, para. 34e)*

Dismayed at state indifference, a broad coalition of NGOs in Mexico and the region submitted the 'Cotton Field' case to the IACHR, which then referred it to its sister institution, the Inter-American Court of Human Rights. The 2009 decision by the Court spurred Latin American women's movements to pressure their governments to have feminicide added to the penal code as a specific offence, or as an additional, aggravating aspect of homicide, just as the Commission's 2001 ruling on the Maria da Penha case gave rise to Brazil's 2006 law on domestic violence. That ruling also provided one of the bases of the Court's judgement.

In early November 2001, the bodies of three young women were found dumped in a cotton field in Ciudad Juárez. Their bodies bore clear signs that following abduction they had been sexually assaulted, tortured, and mutilated. The three had disappeared in the preceding weeks after leaving work. They had been reported missing by their relatives, but the local justice agencies did nothing to locate the victims, preferring to suggest that these young women were off gallivanting somewhere. They also subjected the families to harassment in order to get them to drop their campaign for justice.[8] The 151-page decision noted the longstanding pattern of gender-based violence in Ciudad Juárez as well as the failure of the Mexican state to properly log or investigate these killings, for which very few perpetrators had been arrested, charged, or convicted. It declared that the state had violated the young women's rights to life, personal integrity, and personal liberty, and condemned it for failure to comply with its international obligation to investigate such crimes under the Belém do Pará Convention, which in turn violated CEDAW's requirement not to discriminate.

The judgement broke new ground in a number of ways. It was the first case in an international court to refer to a context of generalised violence and discrimination against women and the first concerning non-state actors engaged in systematic abduction, sexual abuse, and killing of women. It was the first ruling by an international tribunal on femicide/feminicide, terms used, and discussed frequently throughout the written decision.[9] The Mexican state objected to this alleging that it referred to a type of crime that 'does not exist in domestic law or in the binding instruments of the inter-American human rights system'.[10] In fact, Article 21 of Mexico's General Law on the Access of Women to a Life Free of Violence does define feminicidal violence but it came into force in 2007, six years after the Cotton Field murders. The Court's judgement provided the first precedent on feminicide in relation to a binding inter-American instrument and the first piece of regional jurisprudence based on the Belém do Pará Convention. It was also the first assertion by the Court that it was competent to review claims and find violations pertaining to violence and discrimination against women under Article 7 of the Convention. It thereby extended the treaty's enforceability and established the justiciability – that is, the ability of victims to take complaints of violation before a tribunal – of all the rights and protections contained therein. It also laid out unequivocally the international responsibility of states to prevent and properly investigate and prosecute feminicides (Celorio, 2010, p. 638) and emphasised the positive obligations on a state in cases where violence against women was committed by private actors (Tiroch, 2010). The judgement reinforced and clarified the duty of due diligence contained in the Convention, which can only be fulfilled when the state guarantees access to adequate and effective judicial remedies for victims and their families (Abramovich, 2011). These remedies also included reparations to the victims' families, another innovation (Rubio-Marín & Sandoval, 2011). Effective access to justice also implied changes to the institutional attitudes and practices of each state's criminal justice system, an issue taken up in the recommendations of the Model Protocol. Finally, it made a causal link between the social and cultural forms of gender discrimination, gender-based violence, and the indifference of state agencies towards such violence, with all three elements seen as mutually reinforcing. Due diligence in regard to prevention thus requires states to break this linkage by fostering both attitudinal changes and non-discriminatory practices and procedures.

Definitions and Typologies of Feminicide

In the eight years following the Cotton Field judgement, 16 Latin American countries defined feminicide as a distinct crime or an aggravating aspect of homicide. By 2020, every country in Latin America, bar Haiti and Cuba, had introduced the concept of femicide/feminicide into their criminal codes. Of the 32 countries in the OAS, it was almost exclusively the Caribbean ones where the usage of the term failed to gain traction and did not enter law. The first country to act was Costa Rica, in 2007, where Ana Carcedo and Monserrat Sagot (2000) had carried out the first empirically based country study in the region to use this terminology. Costa Rica was renowned for its good governance, stable democracy, and relatively low rates of crime and violence and so this early study was, therefore, exclusively focussed on 'ordinary' intimate partner homicide.

The MESECVI Committee of Experts initially used as a working definition of feminicide:

> [...] the violent death of women for gender-based reasons, whether committed within the family, the domestic unit or within the context of any other interpersonal relationship; committed in the community by any person or committed or tolerated by the State and its agents, through action or omission. (MESECVI, 2008)

Some countries (Bolivia, Colombia, Ecuador, El Salvador, Guatemala, Honduras, Mexico, Nicaragua, and Venezuela) incorporated the Committee's definition of feminicide. Others (Argentina, Chile, Costa Rica, Panama, and Peru) defined feminicide as the murder of a woman by an intimate partner or ex-partner, or as an aggravating factor in some circumstances. When it became clear that some states were defining feminicide rather narrowly as only related to domestic violence, the Committee expanded its definition in 2012 to encompass violence committed 'in the workplace, in public spaces by any person or group of people, whether known or not to the victim' and whether committed 'as an independently defined felony or as an aggravating aspect of homicide'. It also issued the Inter-American Model Law on the Prevention, Punishment, and Eradication of the Gender-related Killing of Women and Girls (Femicide/Feminicide) in 2018, which reflects many of the innovations and principles established in the Cotton Fields judgement.

The region is fairly evenly split in how the crime is given a *nomen juris*. Nine countries (Chile, Costa Rica, Ecuador, Honduras, Guatemala, Nicaragua, Panama, Uruguay, and Venezuela) refer to it as femicide, and eight countries (Peru, Bolivia, El Salvador, Mexico, Brazil, Colombia, Paraguay, and the Dominican Republic) call it feminicide, although the choice of wording does not seem to reflect the earlier debates about the different connotations of these terms. The way that it is included in law also varies (Deus & Gonzalez, 2018). Thirteen countries have a comprehensive law on gender-based violence that defines a wide range of abuses. In seven cases feminicide was criminalised within this law, whilst in four countries it was criminalised in a separate law that preceded (Peru and Uruguay) or followed (Argentina and Colombia) the comprehensive law. Feminicide is specified within the criminal code in twelve countries, and outside of it in the other six. Argentina's Femicide Law does not even mention the word 'femicide' but rather describes it as an aggravating circumstance to homicide. Mexico's law reformed several relevant laws, including the criminal code, whilst Ecuador inserted it in its general criminal code reform prior to approving a comprehensive law in 2018. Five other countries do not have a comprehensive law on violence against women but have criminalised femicide/feminicide in different ways. Brazil, Chile, and Honduras did so through specific laws, the Dominican Republic included it when reforming the criminal code, and Costa Rica inserted it in its law criminalising violence against women.

What, then, constitutes a feminicide in the region's laws? The police, prosecutors, and courts look at a number of elements – victim, perpetrator, context, methods, and motive – and of course there is considerable variation between countries. With regard to victims, every law specifies a woman as the victim, and all the laws except for Bolivia's define feminicide as the killing of a female 'because she is a woman', or for gender-based reasons, which is what distinguishes a feminicide from a female homicide. The key category both for the victim and for the motive – women – seems to assume cis-gender women, as no law mentions transgender women. However, criminal justice agencies are establishing precedents that the category 'women' should be interpreted to include them. For example, Colombia prosecuted its first case involving a trans woman victim in December 2018. Some gender-specific or -related aggravating circumstances also centre on the status and other intersectional features of the victim such as age, disability, or pregnancy, that recognise that vulnerability to violence is multi-layered and complex. These factors were absent in the Cotton Field ruling and only Colombia's feminicide law specifies sexual orientation and identity, poverty, displacement, and minority ethnic status of the victim as additional aggravating factors.

Men are named explicitly as potential perpetrators only in the legislation of Argentina, Honduras, and Nicaragua whilst other countries maintain wording that includes males and females, notwithstanding usages in Spanish such as 'el autor' that supposedly include both men and women. Where the language is more gender neutral, it allows for cases involving lesbian couples. As noted above, some jurists have objected to laws protecting specifically women from violence for violating the constitutional principle of equality. Where men are named as the only possible perpetrators, it was alleged that this potentially criminalised the actor, rather than the act, and thus created *Täterstrafrecht*, a German legal term for offender-based criminal law. This was raised repeatedly in Costa Rica from 1999 to 2007 during the legislative process that led to its feminicide law, and also since 2004 in Spain around its legislation on gender-based violence (Toledo, 2017, p. 49). Some laws also highlight the status of the perpetrator, whether he acted alone or in conjunction with others, held a public office, or had a relationship of authority or hierarchy over the victim. Colombia's and El Salvador's laws provide for an increased sentence if the crime is committed as a group enterprise by two or more people.

The contexts that provide an objective criterion for classifying the murder of a woman as a feminicide nearly always include a relational element between victim and perpetrator. Some countries recognise feminicide only within family relations or intimate partner relationships, and that may be narrowly and formally defined. All countries recognise the context of a past or present intimate relationship in their definition of feminicide. However, the Dominican Republic, Costa Rica, and Chile define feminicide as occurring exclusively within intimate relationships, which in the latter two cases refers purely to formal and cohabiting conjugal relationships. Chile's law criminalises anyone who kills a family member, without regard to the potential power relationships that led to the murder.

In her studies of feminicide in Central America, Carcedo (2010) distinguished diverse contexts, recognising that a view of females as disposable can motivate misogynistic murders of women outside of any domestic or intimate relationship. Her categories of non-intimate and connected relationships between victim and perpetrator (see Table 1) are reflected in some of the region's laws. Although the criminal justice system struggles more to identity murders of women 'by association' as feminicides, motive can also be inferred from contextual information, such as the murder method, the location and the level of excessive, cruel, or sexualised violence employed, that marks the killing as a hate crime.

The region's laws typically fix a penalty for feminicide as an aggravated form of homicide. The penalty may be further increased if additional aggravating circumstances are present, for example, if the murder is carried out in the presence of a family member, following sexual assault, or with ritual violence including mutilation, or includes the dumping and exposure of the body in a public place. Criminal codes also include general aggravating circumstances in homicide cases that can also be invoked when prosecutors request the application of a maximum sentence. These may include the means and level of violence employed in the murder, the motive (beyond misogyny), and the degree of intentionality and planning in the murder.

Table 1.   Types of Feminicide.

	Intimate	Non-intimate	Connected/ Associated
Woman murdered by partner or ex-partner (relationship may be current or prior, permanent or occasional)	X Intimate partner homicide		
Woman murdered by family member (family defined as blood ties or social belonging)	X Matricide, filicide		
Woman killed trying to protect another woman			X
Woman murdered following sexual harassment/stalking having rejected a man's advances and imagined relationship		X	
Sexual murder by man/men known or unknown to the victim, to prevent her identifying the assailant, killed as part of the sexual attack, or left to die of her injuries		Collective rape/murder Serial sexual killers	
One or several women murdered by a stranger		X Serial killer	
Murder of a woman involved in the sex trade (by clients or pimps)		X	
Expression of power or revenge by men against third parties such as members of the same or rival gangs/ crime networks			X

Elaborated by the author, on the basis of Deus and Gonzalez (2018, pp. 18–20) and Carcedo (2010, pp. 14–33).

BRAZIL'S ANTI-FEMINICIDE LAW

Seizing a Legislative Opportunity

Despite the success of the Maria da Penha law in drawing attention to domestic violence, encouraging women to report to the authorities, and prompting improved institutional responses, the number and the rate of murders of women kept rising steadily. In 2007, 3,778 women were murdered, a rate of 3.9 per 100,000, and this had risen to 4,836 women intentionally killed in 2014, a rate of 4.6 (IPEA/FBSP, 2020, pp. 41–42). The final report of the Joint Parliamentary Committee of Inquiry set up in 2012 into the impact and gaps left by the Maria da Penha law detailed a number of feminicide cases brought to the committee's attention. One of the report's 14 legislative recommendations was the immediate creation of a new criminal offence of feminicide

(Senado Federal, 2013, p. 1002), as the next step in the process of judicialising and criminalising gender-based violence. Including feminicide in the Brazilian criminal code had been periodically discussed since the mid-1990s but with little impetus or consensus (Pasinato, 2011). The draft bill included in the Committee's report had been submitted by the SPM, at the initiative of the Mexican director of the UN Women's office in Brasília (Angotti & Vieira, 2020, pp. 55–61). This became Senate bill 292/2013 and was finally approved unanimously on the floor of the Chamber of Deputies on 3 March 2015. Law 13.104 came into effect on 9 March 2015. This was remarkably expeditious for a piece of legislation, for a number of reasons.

Firstly, a group of key actors – the consortium of feminist NGOs behind the Maria da Penha law, the SPM, the *bancada feminina* in Congress, and the lead judicial bodies (CNJ and CNMP) – backed a quick and pragmatic political process that would involve a number of compromises. Feminist activists inside and outside the government were aware, through their participation in other international forums such as the UN, the inter-American system, and the Inter-Parliamentary Union, that Brazil was seen as a laggard, and this sensitivity is evident throughout the Committee's report, and in the justificatory text of various iterations of the bill. Regional experts also participated in the public hearings held by the Committee and in parliament as the bill progressed (Oliveira, 2017, pp. 95–96, 104), which was helpful both in underlining Brazil's international responsibilities and in providing advice on how to word the legislation.

At the same time that Brazil was considering its new legislation, UN Women was looking for a country in which to pilot its Model Protocol for investigating and prosecuting feminicide. Brazil was chosen because of its justice system's capacity to implement a locally appropriate version of the Protocol, the good inter-institutional working relations between different parts of the criminal justice system and other governmental and non-governmental bodies that had been generated by the Maria da Penha law, and the technical capacity of the offices of the United Nations Development Programme (UNDP), UN Women, and the UN High Commission on Human Rights in Brasília to shepherd this process. Thus, Brazilian government institutions began discussing how to implement a law that did not yet exist. In effect, the two processes ran concurrently and created a close working relationship between those sponsoring the feminicide law (the SPM and the women in congress) and the governing bodies of the judiciary (CNJ and CNMP) whose job would be to ensure that it was put into effect. Consultant Wânia Pasinato chaired an inter-institutional working group of 30 professionals from the different agencies of the criminal justice system selected for their technical expertise in either the Maria da Penha law or homicide investigation.[11] Their primary task was the adoption and adaptation of the Model

Protocol, but they also had an important input into the text of the law, thereby removing the lag that so frequently exists between the passage of legislation and practical application of its intent.

The law had to be passed whilst the stars were still aligned in the domestic political environment, with the executive, the two legislative houses, and the judiciary working closely together, assisted by UN Women (Angotti & Vieira, 2020). President Dilma Rousseff, Brazil's first female head of state, was personally committed to prioritising the anti-feminicide bill and her Minister for Women, Eleonora Menicucci, was a close and trusted associate, with strong relations with the women's movement, the *bancada feminina*, and other relevant institutions (Oliveira, 2017, p. 99). But the 2014 elections had been preceded by mass street protests, and opposition forces were gathering. By August 2016, Dilma had been removed from office by an impeachment process orchestrated by the Speaker of the Chamber of Deputies, Eduardo Cunha and her own Vice-President, Michel Temer (Macaulay, 2017). The window for passing the law was clearly closing rapidly.

As the bill moved from Senate to the Chamber of Deputies, the definition of feminicide changed several times, with modifications suggested by a rapporteur's report and two amendments. Changes and substitutions are normal in any legislative process, yet even after the bill had been approved on the floor of the house, the key definition of feminicide was altered at the eleventh hour in a tussle between the *bancada feminina* and the neo-Pentecostal caucus in Congress, reflecting the wider ideological schism at play in the country. The Senate bill PLS 292/2013, issued on 15 July 2013, initially defined feminicide as a form of aggravated homicide, 'an extreme form of gender violence that results in the death of a woman',[12] in one or more of the following circumstances: (I) an intimate affective relationship or family relationship (*relação íntima de afeto ou parentesco*) through blood ties or affinity; (II) any form of sexual violence, before or after the death of the victim; and (III) mutilation or disfigurement, before or after the death of the victim. The bill then proceeded to the Senate's Standing Committee on Constitution, Justice and Citizenship (*Comissão de Constituição, Justiça e Cidadania* – CCJ) for its scrutiny. The CCJ's rapporteurs, Senators Ana Rita and Gleisi Hoffman, approved the bill but with amended wording.[13] Feminicide was re-defined as the murder (or attempted murder) of a woman 'for reasons of gender'. To the specific circumstances outlined in the initial bill was added the use of torture or any other cruel or degrading means. A second amended version was also proposed to the CCJ by Senator Aloysio Nunes. He preferred a phraseology that would encompass murders motivated by a wide range of prejudices such as 'race, colour, ethnicity, sexual orientation, gender identity, disability, social vulnerability, religion, regional or national origin or any other base motive; or in the context of family and domestic violence'. His amendment was rejected as it diluted the intention of the bill's sponsors, which was to give *feminicide* an explicit *nomen juris*.

The bill returned to the Senate for a floor debate in December 2014. Meanwhile the *Procuradoria da Mulher* in the Senate took technical advice on modifications that would enable the law to pass as smoothly as possible. Senator Vanessa Grazziotin, the elected *procuradora*, put forward what would be virtually the final wording. The crime was to be defined as the murder 'of a woman for gender-related reasons', identifiable if committed under two conditions, one, in the context of domestic and family violence and two, with 'contempt and discrimination against women'. The penalty would also be increased depending on the age or pregnancy status of the victim. This streamlined version mirrored the language of the Maria da Penha law, which lays out in detail what legally constitutes domestic violence, thus avoiding the vaguer language of 'an intimate affective relationship' that appeared in the earliest draft. The first condition, of domestic violence, was by then familiar to criminal justice operators and offered a recognisable marker of a feminicide. The second condition concerns *why* the feminicide occurred. The removal of references to *how* a murder is committed – with cruelty, mutilation, torture and so forth – avoided replication of existing provisions in criminal law and opened up the law to wider application.

The bill was accelerated for debate on the floor of the Senate by an incident that demonstrated the growing mood of intolerance. A week earlier, Jair Bolsonaro, then still a lowly backbench federal deputy, declared to a fellow legislator, Maria do Rosário, 'I wouldn't bother raping you, you're not worth it, you're too ugly'.[14] The *bancada feminina* was outraged and demanded that the Senate Speaker show his disapproval by prioritising their bill. The amendment was approved and the bill sent to the Chamber of Deputies as PL8.305/2014. An urgency request was filed which, with a lot of lobbying of the party leaders by the *bancada feminina*, moved it up the legislative agenda.[15] The bill came up for discussion and approval on the floor of the Chamber on 3 March 2015, proposed by Maria do Rosário. It was then that the Speaker, Cunha, a conservative neo-Pentecostal, suddenly demanded a last-minute 'edit', that the key phrase 'for gender-related reasons' be substituted by 'for reasons connected to her being female' (*por razões da condição do sexo feminino*). He told the women's caucus that the bill would not get debated or voted that day unless the term 'gender' was removed. Anxious to get it through in time for International Women's Day, they took a strategic decision and compromised.

It seems that this manoeuvre was Cunha's own initiative and not that of the neo-Pentecostal caucus, which had had months in which to table amendments with alternative wording. He already had a track record of personally sponsoring bills attacking gender-related rights: PL5069/2013 sought to impede access to legal abortion, PL7.382/2010 proposed criminalising 'heterophobia' (there is no law yet criminalising homophobia in Brazil), and PL6.583/2013 set out a 'family statute' that defined the family unit in exclusively heterosexual and nuclear terms. By 2015, the word 'gender' had acquired a taboo quality amongst Brazil's fundamentalist Christians, who associated it almost exclusively with transgender issues, insisting that gender identities were biologically determined, God-given, and immutable. In 2014, a parliamentary debate on the National Education Plan led to them agitating to have mention of 'gender' and sexuality removed from the text, and proposing counter-legislation to ban what they called 'gender ideology' in all education policies and curricula, to the point of threatening to sack or jail teachers who taught about gender.[16] Thus, the substitution of 'sex' for 'gender' in the law was intended to exclude trans women. But this rewording has not restricted justice agencies in their understanding of gender-based violence (Campos, 2015), not least because the Maria da Penha law, which in conceptual and practical terms underpins the feminicide law, refers throughout to 'gender' as a motive for domestic violence (*qualquer ação ou omissão baseada no gênero*).

The Law's Significance and Interpretation

Until 2015, there was no specific mention of the sex of victim or the motivation behind murders of women specifically in the criminal code's provisions on homicide. However, the Maria da Penha law did modify Article 61 of the criminal code, which lays out aggravating circumstances that 'must always lead to a stiffer penalty'. Paragraph (f) was altered to read,

> *if abusing one's authority or taking advantage of domestic relations, cohabitation or hospitality, or with violence against a woman as laid out in specific legislation [viz. the Maria da Penha law].*[17]

This new provision had its effect: a study of 34 jury trials of intimate partner homicides before 2015 notes that in half of the cases, the Maria da Penha law was referred to, primarily when the judge decided the sentence (Machado, 2015, p. 59).

By contrast to the Maria da Penha law, which is an extensive stand-alone law, and to some of the anti-feminicide laws in Latin America, Brazil's law is very parsimonious. That said, many of the features of feminicide explicitly laid out in some of the region's laws are implicit in Brazil's and have gradually been consolidated through jurisprudence and the practical application of the law by the criminal justice agencies, as Chapters Three and Four demonstrate. Brazil's feminicide law alters Article 121 of the criminal code, which defines homicides. Under the heading of 'aggravated homicide' (subpar. 2, VI) it adds an additional category: 'If the homicide is committed...against a woman on the basis of her female sex' (*contra a mulher por razões da condição do sexo feminino*). It then goes on to explain, 'It will be understood that it was on the basis of her female sex if the crime involves (1) domestic violence (*violência doméstica e familiar*) and (2) contempt for or a discriminatory attitude towards women (*menosprezo ou discriminação à condição de mulher*). As an aggravated form of murder, the minimum penalty for feminicide is 12 years and the maximum 30, rather than the 6–20 year range for ordinary homicide. The law also lists some additional aggravating factors specific to feminicide. The sentence for feminicide may be raised by one-third if the victim was (I) pregnant or up to three months post-partum, (II) under 14 or over 60 years of age or had a disability, and (III) killed in the presence of a direct relative (parent, grandparent, child, or grandchild). Defining feminicide as aggravated homicide meant that it also falls under the provisions of the Heinous Crimes law (8.072) of 1990, which covers rape, amongst other crimes, and renders the accused ineligible for bail, or amnesty or pardon once convicted. They must also serve a longer proportion of their jail sentence in a closed prison before being considered for progression to a lighter regime.

The first part of the definition, where feminicide is committed within the context of domestic or family-related violence, is an *objective* measure, that is, the existence of a relationship (real or imagined, past or present) between victim and aggressor is sufficient to categorise a killing as a feminicide, without asking why the perpetrator committed the crime. This part of the definition builds on the Maria da Penha law, which is underpinned by a feminist understanding of unequal structural power relations within the home. The 'why' question in a case of intimate partner or family feminicide is answered by the context: she was killed because society encourages a patriarchal view of wives and girlfriends as possessions to be controlled and disciplined. Criminal justice actors are much more familiar with the objective element of domestic violence due to the Maria da Penha law. Therefore, sometimes investigating police officers, prosecutors, or judges will decide – wrongly – that a murder of a woman is not a feminicide if there is no apparent 'domestic' relationship between victim and perpetrator, sometimes even more narrowly defined as a cohabitational relationship.

Feminicide is distinguished from female homicide by the central question of the *motive* of the perpetrator. The second part of Brazil's definition of feminicide is of an act impelled by a discriminatory and negative emotion or attitude that makes it a hate crime.

Brazilian jurists have debated how feminicide is best characterised when prosecuting the crime. Whilst some argue that the question of motive must be at the heart of understanding a misogynistic hate crime (Bianchini, 2016), there is a risk that asking in court why an individual perpetrator acted as he did opens the door for the defence to deploy well-worn victim-blaming excuses (explored further in Chapter Four). For this reason, the prosecutor's office now refers to feminicide as having an 'objective' character, that is, the motivation of the perpetrator is not personal, but rather conditioned by, and reflective of, structural inequality and misogyny in wider society. The justifications he offers for his violence are not individual to him but constructed by social norms around masculinity and control. His justifications confirm the charge of feminicide, rather than mitigating it. Their position draws on the opinion of an appeal judge who overturned an acquittal in one of the first cases of feminicide committed after the enactment of the 2015 law.

The Brazilian criminal code already contained a number of generic conditions classifying a homicide as aggravated that tend to be included in the charge sheets in feminicide cases. Some relate to motive, such as killing to carry out, hide, escape punishment for, or profit from, another crime, or killing for a trivial reason (*motivo fútil*), or a venal reason (*motivo torpe*). Marineide Freire Ferreira was stabbed to death in the street by her partner on 15 March 2015. The trial judge decided he should be charged not with feminicide but with homicide aggravated by a 'venal motive' as the husband was possessive and did not like his wife working alongside other men. The prosecutor took the case to the appeal court. Justice George Lopes Leite ruled that the aggravated homicide charges of 'feminicide' and homicide for no good reason or a base reason were not interchangeable. Feminicide is motivated by a reason that legislators wanted to make explicit in the law – misogyny and discrimination – which exist as 'atavistic cultural forces' beyond the individual killer.[18]

Although the main aim of the law's drafters was to give feminicide a *nomen juris* as a specific form of homicide, not necessarily to classify it as an aggravated form of homicide, in the circumstances in which the bill was negotiated and this was the easiest way to get it on the statute books (Angotti & Vieira, 2020, p. 51). This had implications for how it would be prosecuted once it reached the judicial system, as Chapter Four demonstrates. The main types of homicide in Brazilian law are simple intentional homicide (*homicídio doloso*), aggravated homicide (*homicídio qualificado*), manslaughter (*homicídio culposo*), and mitigated homicide (*homicídio privilegiado*), for which the best English translation is voluntary manslaughter. In murder cases, the defence team will do its best to get the charges downgraded before, or at, trial to simple homicide or voluntary manslaughter. However, given that feminicide is now defined in law as aggravated homicide, to then argue that it can simultaneously be subject to mitigating factors and somehow presented as a *feminicídio privilegiado* is a legal and logical impossibility for some jurists (Bianchini, 2016). The Latin roots of the word 'privilegio' are 'private' and 'law', thus 'privilege' is a law that applies only to a specific person or a category of person. The 2015 law removed from men the patriarchal privilege of killing women that Segato (2010) argues lies at the heart of feminicide. The law has subjected to public scrutiny and sanction what was previously understood as a private prerogative and broken down the boundary constructed between public and private. That said, it has not stopped defence teams from persisting with such arguments, as will be seen in Chapter Four.

One problem with countries that have criminalised feminicide but lack comprehensive laws is that they are addressing only one aspect of this crime. We will see in Chapters Three, Four, and Five that in Brazil the combination of the Maria da Penha law and feminicide clause in the criminal code encouraged criminal justice agencies to adopt and adapt the UN's Model Protocol, and to develop their own policies and practices to improve the investigation, prosecute, and prevention of feminicide. Chapters One and Two looked at the national political environment and the initiatives of national judicial, political, and civil actors. Chapters Three, Four, and Five will look at how state-level criminal justice agencies – police, prosecutors, and judges – and other subnational actors have responded pro-actively and creatively to the new laws and diffused their innovative responses horizontally, if unevenly, across Brazil.

NOTES

1. See the STF's rulings on ADC 19 and ADI 4424 of 9 February 2012, and rulings (*súmulas*) 536, 542, 588, 598, and 600.

2. The CEDAW committee's report that year urged Brazil to prioritise them.

3. 'Combate à violência doméstica alcança novo patamar com CNJ', CNJ website 12 June 2020.

4. CNJ Resolution 128.

5. The backlog clearance occurs in March, for International Women's Day, in August to mark the month that the Maria da Penha law was passed, and in November to mark the 16 Days of Activism.

6. Portaria 15/2007.

7. The exact name varies from state to state, and some specifically reference violence against women.

8. There is a wide discrepancy in the various data sources with estimates for disappearances of women for the same time period ranging between 400 and 4,500.

9. The Court opted to use the term femicide, meaning gender-based murders of women, for this particular case. Paragraph 137.

10. Paragraphs 139–140.

11. Interview, 3 September 2020.

12. This phrasing echoes that of Article 21 of Mexico's 2007 umbrella law on gender-based violence (*Ley General de Acesso de las Mujeres a una Vida Libre de Violencia*).

13. Ana Rita submitted her report on 18 September 2013, but she then left the Commission and it was not formally approved. Gleisi Hoffman's report of 19 March 2014 largely repeated Ana Rita's wording and arguments. For detail of every stage of the bill's passage see the Senate website https://www25.senado.leg.br/web/atividade/materias/-/materia/113728.

14. He was harking back to a 2003 exchange of words with her in which she had called him a rapist. In 2019, the courts forced President Bolsonaro to apologise and pay damages to her.

15. Generally speaking, around two-thirds of executive-sponsored bills have urgency requests approved, as opposed to one-third of legislative-sponsored bills. The anti-feminicide bill was sponsored by the Senate, but with clear executive support.

16. PL1.859/2015 and PL2.731/2015. This focus on education extended to a movement called *escola sem Partido* ('unbiased schooling'), which also claimed to be eradicating (left-wing) political ideology from educational settings.

17. 'Com abuso de autoridade ou prevalecendo-se de relações domésticas, de coabitação ou de hospitalidade, *ou com violência contra a mulher na forma da lei específica*'. The words in italics were inserted in 2006.

18. Case reference TJDFT Acórdão 904781, 20150310069727RSE.

Chapter Three

RECORDING, RECOGNISING, AND INVESTIGATING FEMINICIDE

INTRODUCTION

Once feminicide was written into law, it was up to the criminal justice system, starting with the police attending the emergency calls and crime scenes, to improve their practices and procedures in recognising, recording, and investigating feminicide. A key stimulus to improvements in criminal justice routines was the launch in 2016 of Brazil's National Gender-informed Guidelines for the Investigation, Prosecution, and Trial of Violent Deaths of Women (Feminicides), hereafter 'National Guidelines', based on the UN Model Protocol (Brazil, 2016). These were the product of three months of intensive multi-agency information sharing and technically informed debate supported, crucially, by the Ministry of Justice and its secretariats for law enforcement and judicial reform. This group opted to issue open-ended advisory guidelines, rather than prescriptive operational protocols, because the next step towards implementation would require individual state justice agencies to produce the latter internally. This approach also avoided push-back from institutions jealous of their autonomy and suspicious of impositions by outsiders. The convenor of the group also insisted that the Guidelines should not just be published and left to sit on a shelf, but also tested and put into practice in five test states following a similar multi-agency process.[1] This assisted some local criminal justice actors in overhauling their criminal justice procedures around feminicide. This chapter starts by showing how the reliability of police data gradually improved due to civil society scrutiny, the action of police entrepreneurs, and evolving understanding of the intersectional dimensions of feminicide. It then analyses how and why the police in some areas of the country managed to refine the quality of their feminicide investigations by setting up case review panels and specialist units and developing local protocols.

RECORDING FEMINICIDE

In 2017, 65,602 people were murdered in Brazil, a rate of 31.6 per 100,000 population, both figures historic highs following a steady rise over a decade, as Table 2 shows. Brazilians represent 14% of all murder victims globally, with a very high rate for a country that is neither conflict affected nor fragile. Therefore, efforts to tackle feminicide must be understood within the context of the country's continuing failure to bring down overall homicide rates until 2018, when there was a marked drop.

Accurate data collection is the first step to designing effective policy, and this remains a challenge in a country with a decentralised criminal justice system whose law enforcement agencies each operate their own databases, constructed with divergent or incompatible criteria, and do not always share results with national bodies. Quantitative data about intentional violent deaths in Brazil are derived from two sources: the Ministry of Health's Mortality Information System, and from the state-level police records. The former always yields a higher number of fatalities, and gives basic information about the victims (sex, age, manner, and often place of death), but nothing about the perpetrator, their relationship with the victim, or their motive. The latter are less comprehensive but give more contextual information about the murder. Despite their discrepancies, the two sources of data track each other closely and female homicide victims have followed national trends.[2] As Table 2 shows, between 2007 and 2017 the absolute number rose by 30.7%, and the rate by 20%.

Prior to 2015, statistics collected on killings of women were very piecemeal (Pasinato, 2011). However, even by 2020, no national justice agency held complete and reliable figures. In August 2019, the CNMP set up a national database (*cadastro nacional*) on feminicide and domestic violence, as mandated by the Maria da Penha law (Article 26-iii), to overcome the problem of data fragmentation. However, so far only 19 of the 27 states have chosen to participate and provide data. Prosecutor's office figures are always lower than those generated from police records, as cases where the perpetrator is dead or unidentified do not show up. In the 85 feminicides committed in Pernambuco in 2018, 13 perpetrators (15%) took their own lives, two were lynched by local people, and two more were nearly lynched and had to be rescued by police. When added to death by natural causes and legal incompetence due to mental health issues, there was no one to prosecute in 20% of the cases.[3]

Table 2. Homicide and Feminicide in Brazil from 2007 to 2019.

	2007	2008	2009	2010	2011	2012	2013	2014	2015	2016	2017	2018	2019
Total homicides[a]	48,219	50,659	52,043	53,016	52,807	57,045	57,396	60,474	59,080	62,517	65,602	57,956	
Rate[a]		26.7	27.2	27.8	27.4	29.4	28.6	29.8	28.9	30.3	31.6	27.8	
Total female homicides[a]	3,778	4,029	4,265	4,477	4,522	4,729	4,769	4,836	4,621 [b]4,793	4,645 [b]4,245	4,936 [b]4,556	4,519 [b]4,340	[b]3,730
Rate[a]	3.9	4.1	4.3	4.4	4.4	4.4	4.6	4.6	4.4	4.5	4.7	4.3	
Feminicides[b]									449	929	1,075	1,229	1,326
% of female homicides classified as feminicide									9.4	21.9	23.6	28.3	35.5

Elaborated by the author.
[a]IPEA/FBSP (2020, pp. 18–19, 36).
[b]FBSP (2020a, p. 116).

From 2015, the most comprehensive national survey of feminicides was that conducted by the FBSP. Its analysis of police crime reports (*boletins de ocorrência* – BO) provided by law enforcement authorities across the country revealed that police recorded 4,556 female homicides in 2017, 4,340 in 2018, and 3,730 in 2019 (FBSP, 2020a, p. 116). Of those 23.6% were logged as feminicides in 2017, 28.3% in 2018, and 35.5% in 2019 (FBSP, 2020a). This rise of 23% in the number of registered feminicides, which contrasts with a drop of 18% in total murders of women, indicates police progress in identifying feminicides rather than an absolute rise in cases. The most recent Global Study on Homicide calculates that family-related feminicides represent 58% of violent deaths of women across the globe, but there are strong regional variations (UNODC, 2019). In the Americas, where the incidence of violent crimes such as drug-related killings and robberies is much higher than elsewhere, the proportion of deaths of women at the hands of family members is relatively lower, at 46% overall, with 35% of all female homicides committed by current or former intimate partners (UNODC, 2019, p. 17). All of the above suggests that the proportion of feminicides identified amongst all female intentional violent deaths in Brazil will likely settle at around 55–60%, the range already reported by state-level law enforcement agencies with the best practices. This means that well over 2,000 women are a year are murdered for reasons related to gender.

There are also wide local variations in incidence, inevitable in a country of continental dimensions. In 2017, São Paulo state had the lowest rate of female homicide (2.2), whilst the northern Amazonian border state of Roraima had the highest (10.6). Over the decade, individual state rates oscillated, depending on several variables. Broadly speaking, the female homicide rate accompanies the general rate in the region and is highest in some of the northern and north-eastern states that experienced sharp rises from the mid-2000s. However, there are too many intervening variables to be able to attribute changes in the feminicide rate to specific homicide or feminicide reduction interventions, and this book does not attempt any statistical, causal analysis, not least because of the wide variance in the way that feminicides are recorded in each state's law enforcement system. For example, in 2018 four states (Federal District, Piauí, Rio Grande do Sul, and Mato Grosso) reported over 50% of female homicides as feminicides. Conversely, many states still record unrealistically low levels, with two of the most violent states (Ceará and Amazonas) registering under 10% (FBSP, 2019, p. 108).

Feminicide Watches

The UN has been concerned about the 'misidentification, concealment and under-reporting of gender-related killings, including of women belonging to ethnic minorities' (UN, 2016, para. 44). Thus, on 25 November 2015, the International Day for the Elimination of Violence against Women, the UNSR called for countries to set up 'feminicide watches', review panels or observatories on 'gender-related killing of women' that would disaggregate the data by the age and ethnicity of victims and by the sex of the perpetrators, note any relationship between assailant and victim, establish risk factors, and propose concrete preventive measures.[4] The need for such monitoring had been highlighted by civil society organisations and by women activists who started to undertake a task that the state was neglecting. In 2012, Karen Ingala Smith set up a blog to chronicle the life of every woman murdered in the United Kingdom, which turned into a Femicide Census in 2015, producing annual analysis of underlying patterns.[5] In Mexico, the highly fragmented criminal justice system forced human rights activists to resort to scouring local newspapers, carefully logging the details of murdered and dumped bodies.[6] The feminicide watch site feminicidiosmx.crowdmap.com and other such initiatives around Latin America and beyond use the same methods (ACUNS, 2017).

Media and civil society in Brazil began to follow suit, building 'social databases' that generally relied on the open source of newspaper reports as police incident reports (BOs) were accessible only to law enforcement officials or to specially authorised researchers.[7] For example, a partnership between researchers at the FBSP, the Centre for Violence Studies at the University of São Paulo, the FBSP, and G1, the online news portal of the Globo corporation, as part of their Violence Monitoring project, produced a snapshot of all the murders reported in Brazil on their portal during one week in August 2017.[8] A team of 230 journalists, covering 500 cities, logged 1,195 violent deaths, of which 126 were of women. They reported on each victim, their characteristics and the nature of their death, with the initial webpage report updated with further news on the police investigation, charges, and prosecution.

This victim-by-victim cataloguing of feminicides continued in a number of states. The #UmaPorUma project in the north-eastern state of Pernambuco was set up on the local multi-media platform *Sistema Jornal do Comércio de Comunicação* by 31 female journalists. Throughout 2018, they carefully documented 241 female homicides, of which the justice system deemed 85 to be feminicides. The individual stories give voice to the silenced victim, detail the impact of her death on her family and friends, and reveal an underlying history of domestic violence that had frequently gone unreported to the police.[9] In some cases, this parallel investigation uncovered vital contextual evidence that convinced the prosecutors to upgrade the criminal charge to feminicide. The profiles also contain details of the progress of the case to trial, giving an insight into judicial processes and decision-making. In the Federal District a very similar project, Elas Por Elas, set up by the award-winning investigative news website Metrópoles, added depth to the news reports assembled by the local Globo team.[10] These independent audit initiatives both helped the general public and policymakers understand the common features of feminicides and underscored the existing gaps in the qualitative and procedural aspects of recording feminicide.

Modifying Police Terminology and Improving Data

The definition of feminicide as a new category of aggravated homicide in Brazil's criminal code required the police and criminal justice agencies to modify their recording practices. Firstly, it had to be differentiated from other homicide categories in police paperwork. The initial crime report (BO) indicates that a crime may have occurred and contains the known facts. Any subsequent police investigation is then handed to the prosecutor's office to bring charges. The BO is the first filter that allows the criminal justice system to 'see' a gender-based assault. Police have a high level of discretion as to whether to fill in a BO or not, what relevant information to include, and how to narrate what is known about the incident after the initial crime scene investigation, forensics, and witness statements. The terminology used in the BO frames how the crime is understood and thus subsequently investigated and prosecuted. However, the fields in the police databases by which the BO is generated are determined locally, either by a department within the civil police or the state law enforcement agency.

It has taken time for local police forces to comprehend the importance of distinguishing murder categories, partly because feminicide is not a distinct crime per se, but an aggravated form of an existing crime (intentional homicide). A survey of feminicides from 2015 to 2017 conducted by G1 and its partners was unable to obtain complete numbers. Police authorities in five states (Amapá, Bahia, Ceará, Maranhão, and Sergipe) responded that they had no data available on feminicides prior to 2017, whilst three states (Paraná, Pernambuco, and Rio de Janeiro) started compiling data only in 2016, nine months after the law changed.[11] One state (Rondônia) claimed it did not log the sex of the victim on the BO, and another (Tocantins) logged murders of women, but did not categorise feminicides separately. In a subsequent survey, in 2018, the data provided to the FSBP by Minas Gerais did not distinguish between manslaughter and murder, and that from Sergipe covered only the major metropolitan region. The largest state in the country, São Paulo, started recording the number of feminicides only in 2018.[12] Many state law enforcement agencies continue to record feminicide in inconsistent and confusing ways.[13]

It took a combination of women's movement and media pressure and the initiative of reformers within law enforcement agencies to transform, state by state, police recording practices. In Rio Grande do Sul, the head of the capital city's DEAM tried for two years to oblige the police Division of Planning and Co-ordination (DIPLANCO) to add feminicide as a BO category.[14] Her recourse to a civil procedure within DIPLANCO had little effect and so in the end she used the leverage of civil society. After a 10-day publicity campaign in October 2017, which saw 400 emails sent to the police chief and the DIPLANCO director, the change was instituted from January 2018, and the state signed up to the National Guidelines.[15] In June 2017, an online campaign, #Issoefeminicidio (#ThisisFeminicide) was launched in several places across Brazil to press for changes in the BO fields.[16] In Pernambuco, a three-month campaign that gathered 4,000 signatures on a petition persuaded the head of law enforcement to remove the term 'crime of passion' from the BO form, replacing it with 'feminicide' by decree of the governor in September 2017, after the state authorities had signed up to the Model Protocol.[17] As the head of the women's policing department noted, using such outdated language in the police investigation reports only helped the defence lawyers to misrepresent this violence in court.[18] Registering a murder as a feminicide in the police-related mortality system now requires stating whether there is known to be any current or past intimate relationship between the victim and perpetrator, any family relationship, or any apparent contempt for the victim expressed through, amongst other things, sexual violence or mutilation of the victim before or after death.

In most states, the murder of a woman is initially put down as simple homicide and changed to feminicide only when the police report is concluded. But this revision depends on the local criminal justice system's technical capacity and motivation. To combat systematic under-categorisation of feminicides, some states adopted a maximalist approach, treating all violent deaths of girls and women as feminicides until the evidence proves otherwise, as both the Model Protocol and the National Guidelines advise. This is important as some murders are set up by the killer to look like a suicide, self-defence, or an accident. In a much-commented case, Tatiane Spitzer fell from the fourth floor of her apartment building in Paraná and it was logged as a suicide until CCTV footage showed her husband assaulting her as they entered the building and forensic evidence proved she was dead before she fell.

The state of Piauí was an early mover and recorded 60% (50 out of 84 cases) of violent deaths of women in 2015–2016 as feminicides. The law enforcement authorities in the Federal District did likewise and registered 60% of female homicides as feminicides in 2018, and 55% in 2019.[19] They also changed the way that disappearances of women are handled: 48 hours after being reported missing they are assumed to be potential feminicide victims, and police mobilisation is swift. In August 2019, Letícia Sousa was abducted from a bus stop on her way to work at the Ministry of Education. Although it was too late to save her, the kidnap squad found the perpetrator, a serial killer and rapist, in just 18 hours by using CCTV footage and interviewing witnesses. He soon confessed that he strangled her because she refused to have sex with him and took them to where he had dumped the body.

An additional effect of this approach was to increase the identification of attempted feminicides. In 2016, before adopting this protocol, Federal District police registered only 16. In 2017, they identified 64, rising to 89 in 2019. Data from a number of sources put the ratio of attempted feminicides to actual feminicides between 2:1 and 4:1.[20] On the one hand, this crime seems harder to classify, as the police need to further establish intent to kill. On the other hand, there is a surviving victim who can give testimony about the assault and events leading up to it. As more women survive murder attempts, due to quicker police response times and improved surgical treatment of injuries, this ratio may increase. This also has implications for how police prioritise cases and work with criminal justice agencies and the local protection network to prevent a further feminicide attempt, and some of the strategies developed are outlined in Chapter Five.

RECOGNISING FEMINICIDES

There is a mutually reinforcing link between recording and recognising feminicide because what is not recognised cannot be recorded, but creating a new category in the record also stimulates the recognition process. The 2015 law helped by specifying a victim (a woman), a primary context (of an intimate/family relationship) and an overall motive (of misogyny). Gradually, data collection has revealed a more complete picture of feminicides and expanded law enforcement agencies' comprehension of how misogyny victimises different categories of women, within and beyond domestic settings.

Victims, Vulnerability, and Intersectionality

Nearly 60% of feminicide victims fall in the age range 20–39 with a median age of 31, reflecting the domestic context, and is older than for male homicide victims, which peaks at age 20–21 (FBSP, 2019, p. 112). In a notable number of cases, the couple has been together for decades before the abuse becomes fatal. In the cases I surveyed in the Federal District and in Pernambuco, the oldest killer was aged 80, with a significant number of victims in their 60s. However, within the universe of feminicides there are also a number of other characteristics that increase vulnerability both singly and in combination.

Race and Ethnicity

Black women are disproportionately more vulnerable than white women, accounting for 66.6% of all killings classified as feminicides (FBSP, 2020a). The murder rate for black women is higher and rising faster, from 4.3 in 2007 to 5.6 in 2017, an increase of 30%, compared to an almost static rate of 3.2 over this period for white women (IPEA/FBSP, 2019, p. 39). There are few in-depth studies, but analysis of 109 feminicide cases in Piauí between 2015 and 2018 reveals that police and forensic examiners recorded 82.5% of the victims as black. However, half of the police records relating to the killers omitted information about ethnicity, making it impossible to draw clear conclusions about racial difference between victim and perpetrator, and thus possible motivation (Villa, 2020, p. 77).

Several overlapping factors contribute to the higher level of victimisation of black women. They are more likely to be assaulted outside the home in hate crimes driven by both misogyny and racism, even more so when combined with further elements, for example, if they are lesbian or transgender, engaged in sex work, or accused of criminal activity. Racism contributes to black women being represented in specific ways, as the subservient maid, as sexualised, promiscuous, and sexually available, as scrounging welfare dependents, and as criminal and untrustworthy, that reinforce a view of them as even more disposable and punishable than white women. They are subjected to additional psychological humiliations, dehumanisation, and controls over their bodies (Carneiro, 2019). Black women victimised in the home or in relationships will face higher structural barriers to leaving the relationship: black women earn 40% less on average than white women and are twice as likely to be employed as domestic workers. Analysis of requests for protection orders in the courts in Rio de Janeiro showed how much black women stressed the precariousness of their financial situation (Bernardes & Albuquerque, 2016). They have less access to education, due both to structural racism and residence in poorer neighbourhoods with lower quality schools. Social service infrastructure is unevenly distributed across cities, with little in informal settlements. When black women do try to access social services, their treatment reveals underlying prejudices. They receive less 'care' from the state because they are viewed as inferior citizens and thus as less entitled. For example, black women are offered less analgesia during childbirth, presumably based on a view that they have a higher tolerance for pain, or simply that their expressed discomfort does not matter. Institutional racism in the police is well documented in many dimensions. Aggressive over-policing of black communities discourages women from reporting to the authorities both because they may be afraid to invite the police into that community due to repercussions by local gangs, and because they do not trust the police to help them. Most of the police staff in the *delegacias* in which they would be filing a report are white, and black women anticipate being dismissed, disbelieved, or humiliated.

The assassination of Rio de Janeiro city councillor Marielle Franco in March 2018 highlighted the violence that women face when their very existence challenges social norms. As a black, lesbian working-class woman with an advanced degree and a political post who dared to openly criticise police corruption and violence, she was murdered to erase all of those aspects of her being. Her suspected killers are police officers closely tied to the Bolsonaro family, and a recent survey of attitudes expressed on social media by Bolsonaro-supporting military police revealed that the top topic of discussion was their resentment at LBGT identities and rights (FBSP/Pulse, 2020). As a hate crime, feminicide is inherently political and intersects with other forms of political and social violence.

Transgender Women

In 2019, 124 trans individuals were murdered, of which 121 were trans women. In only 8% of these cases was there an identified perpetrator, generally an intimate partner. Some 90% of *travestis* and trans women in Brazil survive from sex work, which makes them highly vulnerable to hate crimes (Benevides & Naider Bonfim Nogueira, 2020, p. 29). Yet, their deaths are often dismissed by the police as commercial sex transactions gone wrong, with the unstated implication that the victim was partly to blame. Lynchings of trans women in broad daylight are also not uncommon. In 2017, Dandara dos Santos was beaten, kicked, humiliated, and shot by a group of 12 males (including four minors), for allegedly stealing in her neighbourhood in Fortaleza. Footage of the incident taken by a local drug lord circulated on social media around Brazil and beyond. In April 2018, Jéssica Oliveira was beaten violently with a chair in a lunch bar near Brasília by four attackers, for clearly transphobic reasons. These constitute collectively performed hate crimes whose intention is to physically eliminate what the victims represent in terms of alternative gender identities. The murders are also treated as a form of mass entertainment with images of the killings going viral, as happened to Dandara and to Francisca Gorete dos Santos, whose ex-partner recorded her murder and sent the audio file to a friend who put it up on social media.[21]

Brazil's feminicide law refers to 'women' due to the last-minute removal of the word 'gender' expressly to exclude transgender women. 'Women' could be interpreted from an outdated, purely biological standpoint, or seen as a social – and legal – category of ascribed and/or assumed identity. The social category of *travesti* is longstanding in Brazil and denotes individuals who were allocated male at birth but see, and refer to, themselves as women. They do not demand to be socially recognised as women in the way that trans women do, who generally seek gender reassignment surgery and register their 'social name' (that is, not their birth name) on relevant government documents (Benevides & Naider Bonfim Nogueira, 2020, p. 11).[22] Despite the intention of the conservative legislators, in practice criminal justice agencies understand that both the Maria da Penha and feminicide laws apply to those who self-identify and self-present as women, and will refer to the victim's record of surgery or female name registration if prosecutors, judges, or juries have any lingering doubts.

This working consensus emerged in a piecemeal manner, with the police establishing new working practices before the principle was confirmed in jurisprudence. In early March 2015, just before the law was passed, a police directive in Piauí, defined feminicide as 'the murder of girls, women, *travestis* and trans women for gender-based reasons'.[23] In 2017, Rio de Janeiro police authorities issued an internal directive instructing the women's police stations to assist 'transsexuals who identify as women' in cases of domestic violence, including feminicide.[24] The following year, the state also issued a new Protocol for Dealing with Trans Women and Travestis in the DEAMs, an initiative of the Police Assistance to Women Division (*Divisão de Polícia de Atendimento à Mulher*) and the Municipal Committee on Sexual Diversity (*Coordenadoria de Diversidade Sexual*). In the Federal District, Jéssica Oliveira's became the first such case registered as an attempted feminicide.[25] The police chief overseeing the investigation noted that witnesses heard the group shouting at the victim 'Be a man, be a man!', demonstrating the gender-based nature of the crime.[26] In May 2018, the Federal District's TJ made an unprecedented ruling that cases of domestic violence against trans women fell under the protections provided by the Maria da Penha law and thus could be handled by the Family and Domestic Violence Courts. In 2019, it further ruled that an attempted murder of a trans woman should be considered attempted feminicide.[27]

Women Connected to Criminal Groups

One of the most challenging scenarios for the Brazilian police is when a feminicide occurs 'by connection', in cases where criminal actors kill women who are somehow associated with them. In the north-eastern state of Ceará, the number of young women murdered rose precipitously from 2016 due to four criminal gangs competing for turf for drug dealing and other illicit activities.[28]

In 2018, 114 girls aged 11–19 were murdered, a 322% increase on 2016. In the state capital, Fortaleza, the number of boys murdered in that age group dropped by 40% whilst that of girls rose by 90%, indicating an increase driven by factors untouched by homicide reduction strategies targeted at young men.[29] Once girls were drawn into the ambit of the gangs in their neighbourhood, through male family members or friends, they found themselves monitored and controlled by them, ordered to deliver messages to relatives in jail, and deliver or hide drugs. Some participated actively, whilst others had the misfortune to start a relationship with a young man in a rival neighbourhood or gang. Their relationship to their executioners varied from direct to very indirect. The girls were murdered to settle scores, because they were suspected of being snitches, because they had violated some unwritten gang code about proper female behaviour, such as being 'too mouthy', or because they were considered the property of the rival gang. In many cases their death sentences were announced on social media accounts. The girls were insulted verbally with misogynist epithets suggesting sexual promiscuity (*marmitinha*, *vagabunda*, *safada*, and *pirangueira*) and instructions were given for them to be killed 'with no holding back' (*sem massagem*), that is, with torture and cruelty (Paiva, 2019). The extreme and symbolic violence employed included shaving off hair, scalping, slicing breasts, and rape. In these 'indirect' feminicides, seen very frequently in Central America, the women are seen as completely discardable (Segato, 2010, p. 79). They are *femina sacra*, that is, anyone is allowed to kill them. These young women are 'the waste product' of a communicative act intended to transmit the potential power of men to terrorise all or any women at will, warning them of their fate if they are not careful to avoid members of a rival group. As these girls were murdered for reasons, and in excessive, sexualised, and spectacularised ways absent in the killings of young men, that would qualify these killings as feminicide, yet the gang context has made the local police authorities very reluctant to classify them as such. In 2018, Ceará recorded just 6% of female homicides as feminicides.

The Features of Feminicides

The vast majority (90%) of feminicides in Brazil are committed by current or former intimate partners (FBSP, 2020a, p. 121), with only a minority involving stranger abductions or collective killings. Despite being commonly viewed as spontaneous 'crimes of passion', in reality the timing, the location, and the features of many feminicides demonstrate that they are planned executions. Whilst a majority of feminicides occur between 6 p.m. and 6 a.m. and at home, around 40% occur during the day, when the victim is going about her normal business, with around one-third occurring outside the home (FBSP, 2020a, p. 121; Villa, 2020, p. 142). Indeed, one of the warning signs is heightening stalking by the perpetrator who chooses, or lures his victim to, a situation in which she is defenceless. Women have been killed at the gym, in the supermarket, on a bicycle, on their doorstep coming home from work or college, leaving to take their children to school, and at their workplace. In such circumstances, nowhere is safe. In 2010, Denise Quioca, a civil police *delegada*, was killed in her own office inside the precinct by her former partner, a police investigator, who simply walked in and inflicted 12 gunshot wounds with two service firearms.

Another key marker of feminicide is the means employed. In the Brazilian criminal code, a homicide may be aggravated not just by the motivation but also by the circumstances and the means used, such as denying the victim the chance to defend herself, the ambushing or tricking of the victim, or 'the use of poison, fire, asphyxia, torture or other cruel and insidious means, or which may endanger others'. Whilst firearms are the most commonly chosen weapons in female homicides, in feminicide cases, guns come in second place after knives and other sharp domestic instruments such as machetes.[30] Other methods, such as blunt instrument trauma, strangulation, suffocation, beating, acid and burning are used in lesser degree, but are more typical of feminicide than of homicides committed for other reasons. These methods engage the killer in an extremely physical act of violence, intended to disfigure or obliterate the victim. In some cases, more than one method was employed and 'excessive' violence, beyond that necessary for killing, is a common feature. A victim is stabbed 45 times, another is beaten with a rock, stabbed, and then has petrol poured on her. This performative 'overkilling' is a way of literally inscribing male dominance, control, and entitlement on the bodies of women. Their corpses are also symbolically trashed after the event, thrown into wells, water tanks, sewers and drains, dumped on a dirt track, in a shallow grave, and in the undergrowth.[31]

The 'last chance thinking' typical of domestic feminicide erases both consideration for secondary victims and a desire to escape responsibility (Monckton Smith, 2019). Frequently women are killed in front of children and relatives, some of whom will die trying to fend off the attacker. In an analysis of 33 cases in the Federal District, 28 victims left behind 73 orphans.[32] One element of such murders is what Segato calls horizontal communication between men, with the killer confirming to themselves and other men that they have fully performed a certain kind of masculinity that requires control of women. The main reasons for murder that perpetrators give, when interviewed, are generally a refusal to accept the end of a relationship, or a desire to maintain possession and control (*ciúmes*). Often, perpetrators phone a relative (his or hers) to announce their crime, wait to be arrested, or turn themselves into the police. These patterns of behaviour provide police both with warning signs that can inform prevention strategies (see Chapter Five) and with evidence that killing was motivated by 'contempt and discrimination' regarding women. The investigation procedures developed by a number of police forces have become a lot more adept at recognising these signs of feminicide, enabling them to produce police reports more likely to result in a successful prosecution.

INVESTIGATING FEMINICIDE

One might imagine that feminicide would be investigated by the specialised staff of the women's police stations. But the first DEAMs in São Paulo did not focus purely on gender-based violence, even though the impetus for their creation had been the women's movement demand for a state response to sexual and domestic violence. Their remit was stated in 1989 as investigating 'crimes against females', assisting and referring victims, and enforcing the payment of alimony and child support.[33] A revised decree in 1997 allowed them to investigate murder but only 'in a domestic context and where the perpetrator is known'.[34] After 2006, a number of states passed legislation making the DEAMs' main function to enforce the Maria da Penha law and fulfil the police responsibilities that it outlines. However, in relation to the murder of women, the civil police distinguish between actual and attempted homicide. The DEAMs tend to investigate only the latter, take measures to protect the survivor if the assailant is not in pre-trial detention, and ensure she receives 'humane and specialist' assistance.[35] In a minority of states, such as Pará, Rio Grande do Sul, and Mato Grosso do Sul, the DEAMs do investigate murder. But more often it falls under the remit of the specialist homicide investigation group or *delegacia* in a given locality, or of any generalist police station, if there is no specialist unit. This variable division of labour also affects sexual crimes: in Ceará women had to report rape and other crimes to the women's police stations, but the crime reports would be handed over to the generalist police station where the offence occurred. In 2017, an internal police edict ruled that the women's police stations could now investigate all sexual offences against women, excluding those related to human trafficking.[36]

These practices reveal an entrenched police culture that still sees the role of female police officers primarily as rendering welfare assistance to the vulnerable (women, children, the elderly, and the disabled). The first women to be officially admitted to the police in Brazil were restricted to such duties, and in some states the DEAMs had, or have, such a remit. In 1997, the São Paulo stations had to also take on crimes against children and adolescents, as do those in Santa Catarina currently. It has taken a long time for women to be accepted in all areas of police work, although this has been much faster in the civil police where admission and advancement are much more based on measurable merit and qualifications (holding a law degree is a prerequisite and entry and promotion are by examination). In police organisational culture, dealing with the most serious crimes carries the most prestige. So, for the male and female police officers seconded or volunteering to work in the DEAMs, this posting represents an effective demotion. That said, concentrating feminicide investigations in the DEAMs would still not be ideal due to issues of capacity and distribution. As of 2019, there were only 417 in the whole country, which meant that fewer than 10% of municipalities have a DEAM (IBGE, 2020).

The Model Protocol and National Guidelines emphasised the importance of understanding the different ways in which a feminicide may present, in terms of the victim, motive, circumstance, and perpetrator, and these concerns worked their way into legislation and a reconsideration of police division of labour. In 2017, the Maria da Penha law was modified and Article 12(a) reworded to urge the states, when drawing up plans and policies to tackle domestic violence, to set up not just DEAMs, but also specialist feminicide police units (*Núcleos Investigativos de Feminicídio*),[37] that could combine the investigative expertise of the homicide divisions with the greater experience of the DEAMs in gender-based violence.

In fact, one state, Espírito Santo, had already set up a specialist unit to investigate female homicides back in 2010. Its Precinct for Homicides and Protection of Women (*Delegacia Especializada de Homicídios e Proteção à Mulher* – DHPM) was prompted by concern with the state's very high homicide rate and by the development by consecutive administrations of targeted policies to reduce murders in sub-categories of victims. From 2011 to 2015 the state ran an evidence-led multi-agency approach to violence reduction, *Estado Presente*, similar to those in a number of other states. In relation to gender-based violence, after the state had signed the national pact on violence against women in 2007, criminal justice agencies began to act more strategically. In 2009, the prosecutor's office in the state set up a special unit to tackle violence against women (*Núcleo de Enfrentamento à Violência Doméstica e Familiar contra a Mulher*), training hundreds of police officers across the state, and in 2015 the civil police established an inter-disciplinary unit,[38] bringing together DEAM station chiefs to look at data on gender-based violence and improve their operating practices. These strategies bore fruit: the DHPM reported that in 2019 it had handled 40 cases, of which 17 were classified as feminicides. Of those, police finished their investigations in 16 cases and arrested 13 perpetrators, giving a clear-up rate of 76% (the clear-up rate for all 40 cases was 65%).[39] They also tried not to allow cases to go 'cold'.

In 2019, they arrested 50 suspects, three out of state with the assistance of neighbouring law enforcement agencies. Inter-state collaboration is becoming more common, with suspects apprehended as they flee on highways, or tracked down and detained by partner forces.[40]

The passage of the feminicide law prompted a senior police officer in the north-eastern state of Piauí to pioneer gender-sensitive methodologies in feminicide investigation. Eugênia Villa, a pracademic, policy entrepreneur, and at the time acting head of law enforcement, issued an ordinance on 2 March 2015 establishing the country's first unit to investigate feminicides (*Núcleo Investigativo do Feminicídio*) as well as an inter-institutional centre for research into gender-based violence (*Núcleo de Estudo e Pesquisa em Violência de Gênero*; Neme & Martins, 2018).[41] This centre sought to understand how organisational routines and practices entrenched within the police institution were affecting how the latter handled gender-based violence. The unit also aimed to develop and disseminate practices and protocols that were more gender-sensitive and better able to deliver protection and justice to the victims of violence. The state police authorities had already laid considerable groundwork, offering training in the civil police academy on gender-based violence from 2004, and a course on investigating racially motivated and gender-based crimes from 2012. As soon as the law passed, 'feminicide' was added as a field to the police database. In 2016, the police data analysis centre overhauled the BO and set up a monitoring system to improve data collection and analysis of intentional homicide. When the team heard that Brazil was drawing up National Guidelines, they invited Wânia Pasinato to train local police and Piauí became the first state to sign up.

This interest in using a systematic gender lens led the research group to conduct an in-depth panel review of 27 feminicides committed between March 2015 and August 2016. Police professionals, alongside social science students and academics from the local university, dissected every piece of paperwork related to each case: forensic reports, witness statements, arrest sheets, interrogation of the accused, and the final report. The group used discourse analysis and an organisational approach to understand how the police had been 'seeing' feminicides, what they looked for, what they missed, and what bureaucratic and cognitive shortcuts they had employed to describe and frame the violence. The process was heavily influenced by the Master's dissertation examining police discourses that Eugênia had completed in 2014, and by her doctoral research, which extended her field of study to the discourses of other criminal justice operators. Both drew on Rita Segato's analysis of feminicide as an act of communication, with an audience, and a grammar and vocabulary that are traceable and recognisable. Through detailed case review, police can learn the language of misogynistic violence and how to find its imprint in a crime scene (Villa & Machado, 2018), and how to avoid misinterpretation.

In overlooked crime scene details, they found forms and acts of symbolic violence that indicated a misogynistic hate crime. Knife wounds were concentrated in sexualised body parts such as the genitals and the breasts, and in others that represent emotion or speech, such as the heart and neck. Women were found with items of clothing removed, laid out in the bedroom, or attacked in the bathroom. Violence was often inflicted in highly personalised ways designed to depersonalise and mock the victim: the hairdresser who was scalped, the coconut farmer whose head was split open with her own machete, and the dog collar placed on the psychologist murdered by her own client (Villa, 2020, p. 22). This last case was logged as a violent robbery as the victim's wallet and phone were missing, until CCTV footage showed the killer throwing these items away as he left the scene. It was then charged as homicide. But the dog collar puzzled investigators who thought it might have been used to staunch the blood from the victim's slit throat. Only interrogation of the killer revealed his level of hatred in the act of killing and that bringing a collar to put on her body was a symbolic act of control (Villa, 2020, pp. 284–288).

This analytical approach provided an empirical grounding to the investigative methodology that the state drew up, also reflecting the principles of the Model Protocol and National Guidelines, the Bogotá protocol on improving the quality of homicide data, and Piauí's own forensic investigation manual (Villa, 2020, p. 161). Their method obliges investigators to pay systematic attention to three key elements: the crime scene documentation, how the crime fits into available legal categories, and what material evidence is available on subsequent investigation. Their protocols set out how the autopsy, toxicology screen, DNA collection, and crime scene recording should be conducted. They thus altered the police organisational routine to the extent that, 'Women here trust us to investigate feminicide properly'.[42]

Diffusing Good Police Practice

Good practice in the police tends to diffuse horizontally as a result of organic contact between officers of different forces. Connectors, such as consultant Wânia Pasinato, also play an important role, influencing national actors in the policy forums that they convene, as well as the local actors that they advise and train. Eugênia Villa was also such a catalyst, propagating her feminicide case-analysis methodology across the country. And diffusion can be iterative and multi-directional. Thus, São Paulo state's civil police operating protocol on crime scene documentation inspired Piauí's approach, which in turn helped the former issue even more complete operational guidelines for all stages of police investigation of feminicide (ACADEPOL, 2019; Silvestre, 2020).

However, vertical diffusion and replication of the collaborative multi-agency approach that produced the National Guidelines were trickier. Five states – Maranhão, Piauí, Mato Grosso do Sul, Rio de Janeiro, and Santa Catarina – were selected to adapt the Guidelines to local circumstances. But the results were mixed, as successfully bringing together diverse stakeholders requires a particular alchemy. In Maranhão, a gubernatorial decree established a multi-agency working group composed of representatives of all the criminal justice bodies and the executive branch secretariats for welfare, justice, and human rights. Energetic engagement by the state women's secretariat and local pros-ecutors led to the state establishing a feminicide department within its homicide investigation division in October 2017. In the other states, the process was une-ven or stalled. In Rio de Janeiro, the state's institutions were unable to cohere around the project, despite the presence in the state assembly of Marta Rocha, former DEAM station chief and head of the civil police, whose 2012 protocol for investigating female homicides had informed the national working group. In Mato Grosso do Sul, the judiciary proved to be much keener than the police; and in Santa Catarina, only the military police and forensic investigators creat-ed operating protocols on feminicide. The very different working cultures of the various criminal justice agencies became apparent and representatives on the working groups were more reluctant to critique their own institution's working practices than they had been on the national group. The adoption of standard-ised operating procedures was familiar to the military police, as a hierarchical organisation, but alien to the civil police and to the judicial bodies, where indi-vidual operators act with substantial autonomy and discretion. As a result, these bodies have incorporated the National Guidelines into their working practices in other ways, through published guidance and training programmes.[43]

Where the cognitive and bureaucratic routines of the Brazilian police have undergone the transformations recounted above, they identify and record feminicides more accurately and act more decisively. As perpetrators are inti-mate partners or relatives, they are easily identifiable and often arrested on the spot or shortly after the crime. For example, police data on 107 feminicides committed in the Federal District from March 2015 to July 2020 revealed a clear-up rate of 96%. By law the police must conclude their report within 10 days if the alleged perpetrator is in custody, or within 30 days if not. They are increasingly meeting those targets in feminicide cases. The prosecutor's office also accelerated the filing of criminal charges, which is much assisted by higher quality police investigation reports. However, as Chapter Four will show, the process of getting justice for victims of feminicide slows down con-siderably once the cases enter the court system.

NOTES

1. Interview with Wânia Pasinato, 3 September 2020.

2. IPEA/FBSP (2020) draws on data from both the health system as well as the police records.

3. My case-by-case analysis of the data on the #UmaPorUma site.

4. This reiterated the General Assembly Resolution 70/176 of 17 December 2015 'Taking action against gender-related killing of women and girls'.

5. https://kareningalasmith.com/counting-dead-women/.

6. One such project is Menos Días Aquí. Approximately 1,800 of Mexico's 2,457 municipalities have their municipal police forces. https://politica. expansion.mx/mexico/2019/10/21/carecen-de-policia-650-municipios-otros-cuentan-con-menos-de-15-elementos. Before the 1990s, Mexico had no national official crime reporting system.

7. The discovery of a body will likely lead to a report in the local press. However, even though homicides are the most reliably 'countable' type of crime, this does not take account of disappearances, which may or may not have resulted in a violent death.

8. https://g1.globo.com/monitor-da-violencia/noticia/uma-semana-de-mortes-o-retrato-da-violencia-no-brasil.ghtml.

9. See interviews with the journalists involved in the project at https://www. youtube.com/watch?v=bcIhQqPc7Js.

10. The G1 team in the Federal District maintains a dedicated and regularly updated webpage with profiles of every victim https://g1.globo.com/df/distrito-federal/noticia/2019/12/27/retrospectiva-2019-numero-de-feminicidios-e-o-mais-alto-em-quatro-anos-no-df.ghtml.

11. Eleven states had no data for 2015 and three states had no data even for 2017.

12. http://www.ssp.sp.gov.br/estatistica/violenciamulher.aspx

13. An observation from the FBSP researchers who analyse police data on feminicides for their annual report (FBSP, 2020a).

14. Delegada Tatiana Bastos.

15. https://www.issoefeminicidio.minhaportoalegre.org.br.

16. In Recife, Porto Alegre, Campinas, São Paulo, João Pessoa, and Ouro Preto.

17. https://www.issoefeminicidio.meurecife.org.br. However, this change was enacted slowly. By the end of 2019, the internal police computer database still did not offer 'feminicide' as a search term, but only 'homicide in the context of domestic/family violence'. This excluded non-intimate partner feminicides and appeared to include any victim of domestic violence, male or female.

18. https://jconline.ne10.uol.com.br/canal/cidades/geral/noticia/2017/09/05/feminicidio-agora-sera-registrado-em-boletim-de-ocorrencia-305140.php.

19. Data from http://www.ssp.df.gov.br/violencia-contra-a-mulher/.

20. See Scarance (2017) and data from http://www.ssp.df.gov.br/violencia-contra-a-mulher/.

21. https://catracalivre.com.br/cidadania/no-piaui-homem-e-preso-por-feminicidio-apos-contar-por-audio-a-amigo/.

22. The first gender reassignment surgery was carried in Brazil in 1971 but was not offered through the national health service until 1998 and not regulated by law until 2008. In 2018, the STF and CNJ decided that personal records could be altered by a trans individual without the need for surgery, tests, or medical checks.

23. Portaria 064/GS/2015. The police database allowed for social names to be recorded from 2014.

24. Resolução SESEG No.1110 4 August 2017.

25. It was handled by a special police precinct that deals with discrimination on the basis of race, religion, sexual orientation, disability, or age.

26. https://g1.globo.com/df/distrito-federal/noticia/policia-do-df-investiga-tentativa-de-feminicidio-contra-mulher-trans-entenda.ghtml.

27. https://www.uol.com.br/universa/noticias/redacao/2019/08/10/violencia-contra-trans-tambem-e-feminicidio-decide-tribunal-no-df.htm.

28. The number of women murdered in the state has quadrupled in a decade, from 117 in 2008 to 475 in 2018 (IPEA/FBSP, 2020, p. 41).

29. https://www1.folha.uol.com.br/cotidiano/2020/01/com-decretacoes-via-rede-social-assassinato-de-meninas-dispara-no-ce.shtml.

30. Analysis of 2019 microdata from 19 Brazilian states indicates that firearms were used in 72.5% of all homicides, but only in 26.9% of feminicides. Knives were used 53.6% of cases (FBSP, 2020a, p. 121).

31. All real examples from the cases documented in the Federal District and Pernambuco.

32. Elas por Elas project, in Metrópoles.

33. Decree 29.981 of 1989.

34. Decree 42.082 of 1997.

35. See, for example, Article 2 of Portaria 476 of 2017, issued by the Office of the Chief of Police, in Goiás state.

36. Portaria 231/2017.

37. By Law 13.505.

38. Núcleo Interdisciplinar de Estudos e Elaboração de Ações para o Enfrentamento à Violência (NIEV).

39. https://www.es.gov.br/Noticia/ balanco-da-dhpm-50-suspeitos-de-homicidios-contra-mulheres-detidos-em-2019.

40. Based on my reading of cases in Pernambuco and the Federal District, and the CNJ's annual push to bring cases to trial, detailed in Chapter Four.

41. Portaria 064-/GS/2015.

42. Personal communication.

43. Interview with Wânia Pasinato, 3 September 2020.

Chapter Four

PROSECUTING AND PUNISHING FEMINICIDE

INTRODUCTION

On 13 November 2006, Paulo Eduardo Costa Steinbach saw his wife with a man he took to be her lover. An argument ensued, and he drove his car at her, crushing her against a wall, witnessed by the two children (their son and her daughter) with him in the car. The victim, Yara Margareth Paz Steinbach, died in hospital of her injuries. The killing, in the southern city of Florianópolis, occurred just months after the Maria da Penha law had passed and expectations were high that this case would be dealt with promptly and in an exemplary fashion. But justice for Yara turned out to be slow and partial.

The trial took place a decade later, during which time the killer spent just one year on remand, as his lawyers had used every legal loophole available to avoid prison.[1] Their various habeas corpus petitions, which they escalated from the state appellate court (TJ) to the Supreme Court of Justice (*Superior Tribunal de Justiça* – STJ), and even to the Federal Supreme Court (STF), alleged that he did not represent a threat to public order, questioned the charge of homicide aggravated by surprise rendering the victim defenceless, queried the competence of the Family and Domestic Violence Court to hold the preliminary hearings establishing probable cause, and alleged that one of the TJ judges had a conflict of interest as he had acted as a prosecutor in a hearing on another of their petitions. The defence team also twice filed to prevent the trial going ahead (in 2010 and 2016). When the case was eventually heard, the jury and judge accepted the defence lawyer's mitigating argument that Paulo had acted under the influence of 'powerful emotion' (*violenta emoção*) because he saw his wife cheating on him. He claimed that he had forgiven her for cheating once before, and that he had not intended to hit her with the car.

He was found guilty of *homicídio privilegiado* and received a prison sentence of five years and four months to be served in a half-way house. The prosecution appealed against the jurors' majority decision that she had not been taken by surprise, arguing that just because she was standing in the street arguing she could hardly have anticipated that he would run her over, as the defence had posited. The TJ disagreed.[2]

This case illustrates many of the problems that beset feminicide cases once the police investigation is concluded and they proceed for prosecution and trial. The problems are of two orders. The first consists of the delays attributable to procedural and bureaucratic features of the Brazilian criminal justice system. The second obstacle to justice concerns the way cases play out in court. In the judicial phases of a case, the relevant actors are the prosecutors, defence lawyers, judges, witnesses, and jurors, whose underlying attitudes shape how the act of feminicide, its victim, and its author are presented and understood, and determine what will happen to the perpetrators. Both of these problems, as we will see, have been addressed by the justice institutions and policy entrepreneurs within them.

This chapter details the legal, institutional, and cultural shifts occurring, and still needed, in the way that feminicide cases are tried in Brazil. The first section examines why it takes so long for them to come to trial. The time lag is due to slowness and inefficiency in the courts and to defence lawyers deliberately employing all available delaying tactics. The next section examines what happens in the courtroom. It outlines the peculiar features of jury trials in Brazil and how this affects outcomes, as jurors respond to the alternative narratives proffered by the defence and the prosecution. The most common exculpatory strategies are examined in the light of how social attitudes to feminicide have changed in the last few decades, in response to women's movement pressure and to key court rulings on what is a permissible defence argument. It shows how the specious 'honour defence' has been discredited, but the arguments of provocation and temporary loss of reason continue to be deployed, resulting in acquittals. The final section examines the various initiatives undertaken by the national judicial authorities to speed up trials and improve conviction rates in feminicide cases through institutional capacity building.

JUSTICE DELAYED, JUSTICE DENIED: GETTING FEMINICIDE CASES TO TRIAL

Once the civil police have concluded their investigation into a feminicide, the file is handed over to the prosecutor's office (*Ministério Público* – MP), which then decides which charges (*denúncias*) to bring against the accused. The crime and aggravating elements of the criminal code listed on the charge sheet may not always be the same as those indicated in the police investigation. On balance, the prosecutor's office is slightly more likely to classify a killing of a woman as a feminicide, possibly because it has an institutional interest in seeking maximum sentences.[3] When those charges have been formally filed and the judge has received the prosecutor's recommendation, the case proceeds to a pre-trial hearing (*audiência de instrução*). The judge hears the accused and witnesses on both sides and may subpoena additional witnesses or seek further evidence to determine probable cause. The judge's *sentença de pronúncia* then confirms that an indictable offence appears to have been committed and the case goes to a jury trial.

On average over a year elapses in feminicide cases between the charging of the accused and the jury trial.[4] The notorious sluggishness of the Brazilian judicial system is the result of a number of factors. One is simple bureaucratic inefficiency, that is, cases getting stuck in a drawer somewhere (and for that reason is called *tempo de gaveta*), awaiting a minor action, such as tracking down a witness or chasing a piece of evidence from the forensic lab. This kind of holdup accounts for around 80% of delays in proceedings.[5]

Another factor is case overload relative to the number of court staff, as more and more criminal offences have been added to the statute book. The National Justice Council's data for 2018 showed that there were over 78 million cases pending in the court system, of which 9.1 million were criminal cases (CNJ, 2019b). On average criminal cases were taking nearly four years to move through the system, although jury courts were less backed up than other courts, as they deal only with the more serious crimes against life. Brazil's code of criminal procedure also allows defence lawyers to use legal loopholes and technicalities and to file multiple petitions as delaying tactics (*recursos protelatórios*) in the hope that the statute of limitations (*prescrição*), which is 20 years for homicide cases, will cause the case to time out. These also clog up the court system.

It was such delaying tactics employed by her ex-husband in an attempt to dodge justice that had led to Maria da Penha to take her case to the IACHR. At his first trial for attempted homicide in 1991, he was sentenced to 10 years in prison. However, the appeals lodged by the defence led to the verdict being annulled, and a second trial took place in 1996 in which he was again sentenced to prison. Once more, he walked free, as the defence alleged procedural irregularities in the trial, and their appeal languished in the TJ.[6] The IACHR's 2001 report considered that justice delayed in this way was effectively justice denied. The Commission noted that 'the police investigation completed in 1984 provided clear and decisive evidence for concluding the trial' and that the delays in court proceedings were unwarranted by 'the characteristics of the case, the personal situation of persons involved in the proceedings, the level of complexity, and the procedural action of the interested party' (IACHR, 2001, para. 39). These had denied her access to 'the prompt and effective remedies', including the right to civil damages, to which she was entitled under the American Declaration of the Rights and Duties of Man and the Belém do Pará Convention.

These delaying tactics were also facilitated by some peculiarities in the Brazilian criminal justice system. One is that the federalised system of government means that the accused can appeal not just to the TJ, but also to the STJ and the STF. In most countries, the Supreme Court would be an exclusively constitutional court, dealing with test cases on matters of legal principle. However, Brazil's STF also acts as the court of last instance for the entire judicial system and handles cases in which there was no issue of jurisprudence at stake, but where a constitutional violation is alleged.[7] In order to reduce the burden on the STF, in 2004 constitutional amendment No.45 introduced two filters: the principle of binding precedent whereby any decision agreed by two-thirds of the court would oblige all lower courts in the country to follow suit on the issue in question, and the 'general repercussion' principle, intended to avoid repeatedly ruling on identical issues. Some key rulings have been made since then of matters relating to the prosecution of feminicide cases.

Procedural delays, and apparently unduly lenient outcomes in feminicide cases, were also uppermost in the minds of the authors of the Joint Parliamentary Committee of Inquiry report that proposed the feminicide bill in 2013. The top tiers of the justice system took on the IACHR's message that hold-ups of several years in trying feminicide cases were unacceptable. Brazil's National Guidelines instruct judges to disregard or quickly deal with attempts by defence lawyers to game the system, which they began to do more vigorously (Brazil, 2016, pp. 106–107). For example, Roberta Viana Carneiro was murdered in Ceará in December 1998, and her then partner found guilty in December 2007. There ensued 11 years of appeals to the TJ, the STJ, and the STF. In April 2019, the Prosecutor General, Raquel Dodge, counterfiled and obliged the STF justices to order the perpetrator to start serving his prison sentence immediately. She also slapped a fine on him for 'vexatious litigation'.[8]

The current statute of limitations on forms of gender-based violence is clearly problematic in the light of such delaying tactics. One argument made for a period of proscription is that it protects the accused from the perverse inefficiency of Brazil's legal system. But this same inefficiency also denies justice to the victims and their families. Thus, on 6 November 2019, the Brazilian Senate unanimously approved Constitutional Amendment No. 75 which would add both rape and feminicide to the list of crimes for which the accused is ineligible for bail (*inafiançável*), and for which charges cannot lapse due to time expired (*imprescritível*).[9] The bill will need to be approved by the Chamber of Deputies.[10] Although the author of the bill, Senator Rose de Freitas, noted that this would assist in cases where the perpetrator had absconded, on which courts and police are beginning to take more co-ordinated action, the impact is likely to be greater in terms of dissuading defence lawyers from pursuing ultimately fruitless strategies.

FRAMING FEMINICIDE IN COURT: JUDGES, JURIES, AND DEFENCE STRATEGIES

Once a murder case enters the judicial system, defence lawyers immediately try to have the charges presented by the prosecutor's office dismissed or reduced. One aim is to avoid a jury trial, which in Brazil is used exclusively to try intentional crimes against life.[11] Alternative charges, such as bodily injury followed by death (*lesão seguida de morte*), rape resulting in death (*crime de estupro com resultado morte*), or manslaughter (*homicídio culposo*) would be heard before a judge. The first opportunity to query the charges comes at the evidentiary hearing, where a presiding judge will hear the defence, the prosecution, and key witnesses. The defence lawyer will also challenge the classification of the crime as feminicide because this is a form of aggravated homicide that automatically attracts a heavier sentence. The charge sheet will almost certainly list additional aggravating features related to motive (even though alleging a 'base' or 'insignificant' motive is arguably redundant alongside a charge of feminicide), method (surprise and cruelty), specific vulnerability (age and pregnancy), and whether the murder was committed in front of a direct family member.

In the preliminary hearing and the jury trial, judges, defence lawyers, and prosecutors are all engaged, consciously or not, in framing the perpetrator and the victim in their questions and arguments and often invoke society's tendency to hold binary views or archetypes about opposing poles of masculinity and femininity (Corrêa, 1981, 1983). If the perpetrator can be portrayed as an honest breadwinner and dedicated family man, and his use of violence as an aberration, provoked by exceptional circumstances, acquittal is more likely. Conversely, the ideal female victim for the criminal justice system is the unimpeachable housewife, the obedient daughter, the studious schoolgirl. In one preliminary hearing, the judge asked a witness about the victim, 'Did she have a routine for going to work, taking the children to school? Was she a responsible person? Well-balanced?' (Machado, 2015, p. 46). Witnesses also fall into this need to present the victim as completely 'innocent' and blameless.

When feminicide cases come to trial, the prosecutors have to deal with another significant variable, which is the pre-existing attitudes of the jurors and of the judge towards violence against women. Courtrooms are theatres, in which the defence lawyers and prosecutors choose argumentation strategies intended to sway the jurors with their performance and play on their prejudices and preconceptions (Schritzmeyer, 2013). Given the explicit expectation in Brazilian law that jurors will vote according to their inner conviction, or how they *feel*, both sides make efforts to appeal to jurors' 'commonsense' views of intimate relations and gender roles.

Jury Trials in Brazil

The mechanics of jury trials in Brazil's civil law system are quite distinct from those of the Anglo-Saxon common law system.[12] There are only seven jurors, referred to collectively as the Sentencing Council (*Conselha da Sentença*). Throughout the trial they are not allowed to confer with one another. At the end of the presentation of evidence by the defence and prosecution, each juror is called, one at a time, into a special room where they are required to give simple yes or no answers to a series of questions (*quesitos*) drawn up by the judge in conjunction with the defence team and the prosecution. These *quesitos* follow a standard sequence laid out in Article 483 in the code of criminal procedure, although their content will reflect the specific facts of the case. The questions ascertain the juror's personal conviction in relation to the following: whether the crime occurred, who committed it, whether the accused should be acquitted, whether there are any mitigating circumstances, and whether there are any aggravating circumstances. If three or more jurors answer 'no' to the first two questions, then the accused is acquitted. If three or more jurors answer 'yes' to the first two questions, then they are asked if the accused should be acquitted.[13] The sequence of questions was streamlined in 2008, in an attempt to simplify the procedures and avoid unclear outcomes. However, it is still possible for jurors to give apparently contradictory answers to these questions, particularly in relation to the third, when the majority vote is to acquit even if the authorship of homicide, aggravated or not, is accepted. The defence's exculpatory arguments are key in influencing the response to that question.

The reasons this situation can arise are that in Brazilian legal culture and process a distinction is drawn between the role of the judge and that of the juror. It is presumed that judges, on the one hand, who have extensive legal training, will base their verdicts on the law as it is written, or at least on a jurisprudentially justifiable interpretation and application of the law. They have freedom and autonomy in that interpretation, but it must be based on the law, in what is termed *livre convencimento motivado*. Jurors, on the other hand, are presumed to have no legal training and no expert knowledge of the law. They are expected to act upon their own personal conviction (*íntima convicção*), their conscience, and personal sense of justice. This explains why the jurors do not confer. In the Anglo-Saxon 'Twelve Angry Men' scenario, the jurors furiously debate the balance of evidence, in an attempt to come to a consensus as to whether the accused is guilty 'beyond reasonable doubt'. They are not seeking an absolute or knowable truth about what happened, but rather looking at the information revealed in the available evidence. In the Brazilian system, largely derived from Portuguese civil law and related to the Romano-Germanic legal tradition, the jurors vote on the *quesitos* according to their idea of the 'truth' of a situation, based on their understanding of the social context that produced the behaviour on trial. That 'truth' is, of course, a construction or an expectation strongly shaped by social norms, in this case, prevalent ideas about power relations between men and women, and the acceptability of violence in highly gendered contexts. As Schritzmeyer (2013) observes, every jury session is a test of the world of moral, social, and economic rules. The contrasting roles of the judges and jurors are summed up in a dissenting opinion in the STJ's landmark 1991 ruling: 'Judges apply the law to the man: jurors apply the man to the law' (Pimentel, Pandjiarjian, & Belloque, 2006, p. 112).

Exculpatory Strategies: 'Honour', Emotion, and Provocation

The criminal code contains a number of articles that offer the possibility of acquittal, of a lower sentence for a *homicídio privilegiado*, or of a higher sentence for homicide that is aggravated in various ways. In feminicide cases, the defence team will pursue the first two options and try to avoid the latter, by arguing either that the violence committed was necessary and legitimate and therefore not a crime, or that the violence was committed as a result of an altered emotional state (immediate or long term), which means that the perpetrator should be considered less criminally responsible. Whilst the two lines of argument are distinct in terms of the articles of the criminal code that in theory sustain them, for practical and persuasive purposes they are inter-linked. They both suggest that the victim is to blame, by forcing the perpetrator to 'defend himself' or by causing his altered emotional state. These are presented as reactions with which an average person could empathise. Fortunately, the social comprehensibility and excusability of lethal violence against women have been eroded over the last couple of decades by feminist campaigning, the passage of new laws, key pieces of jurisprudence, and concerted institutional efforts by judicial bodies.

Up until the 1990s, acquittal in feminicide cases hinged on appeals to Article 23 (2) of the 1940 Criminal Code, which still stands in its 1984 revised version. It states that an act has exemption from criminal prosecution (*excludente de ilicitude*) if it is committed in legitimate defence. Article 25 defines legitimate defence as 'the reasonable use of the necessary means to fend off an unwarranted attack, ongoing or imminent, on one's right or that of others'. What is curious in this definition is that it does not refer, as one might expect, to physical self-defence in the context of imminent threat to life but rather to the vague category of a 'right' under attack. But which 'rights' can be legitimately defended with reasonable use of force is not defined. To what does a man have a right? To an intimate relationship from which his partner cannot withdraw? To a partner who is faithful, or respectable, or uncomplaining, or who behaves as he dictates? Nowhere in this clause is the word 'honour' used: the term appears only in another part of the criminal code in relation to defamation and insult. Nonetheless defence lawyers have used this clause to argue that a wife's infidelity – or other kinds of supposedly outrageous behaviour – had a damaging effect on the husband's honour. Implicit in this argument is the idea that a man has a 'right' to untarnished honour and that his social standing hinges on his ability to control his partner.

This notion of honour has deep cultural and legal roots (Corrêa, 1981). Until Brazil's independence in 1822, Portuguese colonial law explicitly permitted a man to kill his wife and her lover if he caught them in the act of adultery. Brazil's first post-independence criminal code of 1830 removed that provision but the notion that murder was a legitimate response to spousal infidelity lingered discursively in courts well into the twentieth century, assisted by the collusion of the justice system and the fact that adultery remained a crime on the statute books until 2005. The following criminal code of 1890 introduced an alternative *excludente de ilicitude* for spousal murder, allowing that it was not a crime if committed 'in a state of total perturbation of the senses and intelligence'.[14] It was implicit in this clause that behaviour by a woman that besmirched her husband's honour would cause him to lose his mind. A study of trials of men who got away with murdering their intimate partners in Rio de Janeiro between 1890 and 1930 showed that in every case they were acquitted on the grounds that they were defending their 'masculine honour', an argument that relied on the new temporary loss of reason clause (Engel, 2000, p. 169–170).

However, this legal and societal indulgence towards 'crimes of passion' prompted something of a moral panic about a perceived surge in cases, evidenced in coverage by popular women's magazines of the era (Besse, 1989).

This led to a coalition of – all male – prominent prosecutors, judges, criminologists, social hygienists, and forensic examiners who launched a campaign against acquittals on such grounds, especially in regard to wife murders. Whilst female commentators of the time had been concerned about women's safety, these legal experts saw this permissiveness towards violence in the family sphere as contrary to the modern, civilised, reasoned, and healthy society they hoped Brazil would become. In the short term, their actions resulted in a much higher number rate of conviction and jail terms in cases of intimate partner homicides (Besse, 1989, p. 655). In the longer term, they claimed credit for a revision in the third criminal code of 1940 that downgraded the temporary loss of reason argument from one of exculpation to one of mitigation: it could reduce the sentence, but not lead to the charge being dismissed (Eluf, 2007, p. 164).

After 1940, legal and public concerns about this issue faded away, but defence lawyers continued to rely on a dual appeal to defence of honour and temporary loss of reason to argue for acquittal, not just mitigation, as a study of feminicides in the 1950s and 1960s shows (Corrêa, 1983). The criminal code was revised again in 1984, the year that Brazil ratified CEDAW. The select group of (again, all male) jurists who revised the code apparently 'took a lenient view towards crimes of passion' and left contradictions and defence loopholes (Human Rights Watch, 1991, fn 28). Article 28 (1) follows the 1940 code in stating clearly that 'emotion or passion do not constitute an exemption from criminal responsibility'.[15] Yet, Article 121 on homicide allows mitigation if the crime is 'motivated by relevant social or moral values, or driven by violent emotion' and this language was inserted in the 1984 revision of the code, in Article 65, as a general mitigating provision. A charge of *homicídio privilegiado* allows the normal murder sentence of six to twenty years to be reduced by a sixth to one-third. As the minimum sentence for homicide is a six-year jail sentence, a one-third reduction brings that down to four years. According to Brazilian law, first time offenders serve any jail sentence of four years or less in a special half-way house, where they spend only their nights and days off, and they can work or study. There are very few of these hostels in Brazil, so in reality the sentence is served in the offender's own home. This meant that before 2015 many men convicted of killing their female partners spent little or no time in jail, for generally they awaited trial at liberty, often for years.

The abstract concepts on which criminal law is based are inevitably subject to interpretation that is culturally, temporally, and spatially rooted. But that interpretation is also mutable and open to challenge, by social movements, academic studies, legislation, and jurisprudence. The key concepts mitigating feminicide are 'emotion' and 'passion'. Brazilian jurists have distinguished between powerful emotion, understood as a spur of the moment, fleeting sensation, and deep passion, which is defined as obsessive, deep-seated, enduring,

consuming, and corrosive (Eluf, 2007). The former would be used, in principle, to argue temporary loss of reason and self-control. In fact, the current
criminal code leaves the door open for both kinds of response to be used in
mitigation. Article 121, on homicide, allows for 'violent emotion *immediately
following* provocation on the part of the victim', whereas Article 65 omits the
words 'immediately following', thus allowing that the aggressor's obsessive
paixão, supposedly provoked by the victim, could come about days, weeks,
or months later. The debate about 'crimes of passion' in the 1920s and 1930s
in Brazil hinged precisely on whether this kind of delayed and vengeful reac-
tion could be excused as temporary insanity. Roberto Lyra, a leading jurist
who campaigned for a change in the criminal code, noted that these crimes
were often pre-meditated and planned, and therefore could not be excused
using appeals to loss of reason (Lyra, 1935). This is still the case. 'Crimes of
passion' is a pseudo-legal term, as 'passion' is mentioned in only two places
in the criminal code, in a clause related to the abuse of vulnerable people
without full capacity (*paixão* here refers to their attachment to the abuser)
and in the clause stating that emotion and passion provide *no* defence against
criminal responsibility. The word that appears often on the police incident
reports to describe motivation in spousal murder cases is *ciúmes*. The Latin
root means both zeal and jealousy and covers a wide range of feelings – pain,
rage, sadness, envy, fear, depression and humiliation, obsessive thoughts, and
even physical symptoms. The Latin root of the word passion is suffering. So,
a 'crime of passion' is, in reality, an act not of love but of control, committed
to rid the perpetrator of uncomfortable and painful feelings by eliminating the
person he regards as the source of the feeling and, often, himself.

Defence strategies often invoke a complex moral economy of emotion. The
underlying logic of the 'powerful emotion' argument is that no reasonable
man would murder his wife. The notion of 'unfair provocation' has simply
substituted for the idea of honour under attack. The language is different, but
the meaning is the same: 'she made him do it' (Hill, 2019). And what kinds of
behaviour might constitute 'unfair provocation'? Dancing with another man?
Asking for a divorce? Powerful cultural and social norms around domestic
violence and 'honour' deliver a message: that the abuse and murder of women
is actually reasonable and justifiable, as a means of men achieving a particular kind of masculinity that relies on power of life and death over women
(Segato, 2010). The degree to which the jury finds the violence 'understand-
able', and thus reasonable in the context of social norms, is what is at stake in
feminicide trials. The case of Yara Steinbach above illustrates the slipperiness
of these arguments. The accused claimed he did not mean to kill her with the
car, he was merely trying to reverse the car to drive away, in which case her

death was an accident or manslaughter (the charge his lawyers tried to get it changed to).[16] Yet, by arguing that he acted out of powerful emotion, that is, rage when he saw his wife with another man, the defence lawyers were in fact telling the jury that he *did* intend to kill her, but with the red mist as a mitigating factor. The prosecutor in the case, Luiz Fernando Pacheco noted, in frustration, 'Cheating does not constitute licence to kill'.[17]

Jurisprudence and Changing Judicial Attitudes

The 1970s and 1980s continued to see many acquittals of men who murdered their intimate partners. However, one case would forever change the public debate, as it enabled women's groups and feminist jurists to challenge and deconstruct the notion of feminicides as 'crimes of passion'. On 30 December 1976, Ângela Diniz, a wealthy socialite, was at her beach house in the chic resort of Búzios, near Rio de Janeiro. That day she had informed her boyfriend, Raul 'Doca' Fernando do Amaral Street, of her intention to end their relationship. He packed his bags and drove off. However, he returned unannounced later that evening, tried unsuccessfully to change her mind about the relationship, and a violent row erupted. She attempted to flee to the bathroom, but he pulled out a revolver and killed her in the corridor, shooting her at point blank range in the face.

The trial by jury was held in 1980 in Cabo Frio, the jurisdiction where the murder had occurred. The accused's defence lawyer was Evandro Lins e Silva, a very eminent jurist at the end of his career who used this notorious case as his swansong. His defence strategy consisted of well-worn arguments about the supposed co-culpability of the victim.[18] In his address to the jury, Lins e Silva argued that,

> [...] the victim always has some hand, to a greater or lesser extent, in setting off the tragedy that unfolds. This chap acted out of passion, he committed a crime due to circumstance, he is not a habitual criminal. His act of violence was an isolated act in his life, the result of a moment of madness and despair .... When love becomes obsession ... a man is overwhelmed by jealousy and becomes the slave of passion and ends up being subjugated by the object of his affection.

The court did not accept the characterisation of this murder as a 'legitimate defence of honour' but agreed that Street had acted 'under the influence of violent emotion'. The jury convicted Street of a lesser charge of excessive force that resulted in a two-year suspended sentence. This prompted uproar, and feminist groups took to the streets with banners proclaiming, 'Those who love don't kill'. Prosecutors challenged the verdict the following year and the TJ annulled it. The re-trial in 1981 convicted Street and sentenced him to 15 years in prison, of which he served five behind bars.

This case prompted the women's movement to mobilise against such acquittals and they won a victory in 1991, when the honour defence was demolished jurisprudentially. In 1988, in Apucarana in Paraná, João Lopes had tracked down his wife to a hotel and stabbed to death both her and her lover. His acquittal in the local court went to appeal in the STJ, which annulled the verdict. The highest criminal court in the land ruled that a man's honour cannot be injured by his spouse's adultery because honour cannot exist in a conjugal context, that is, *between* people. Honour is a personal, non-transferable attribute that can be maintained, damaged, or lost as a result of one's *own* actions but not by the actions of third parties. Furthermore, the decision noted that civil law allows for separation and divorce, and nothing can justify killing a spouse who has damaged her own honour.[19] This ruling satisfied General Recommendation 19 of the UN's Committee on the Elimination of Discrimination against Women, which the following year urged States Parties to enact 'legislation to remove the defence of honour in regard to the assault or murder of a female family member' (CEDAW, 1992, para. 24r).

Yet, Lopes was again acquitted in the re-trial in the local court because, in the absence of the principle of binding precedent at that time, lower courts were not obliged to follow the rulings of upper courts. Defence lawyers continued to invoke the honour defence, forcing the STJ to reiterate its position. In 2001, the STJ overturned the acquittal of a man who had murdered his wife, from whom he had been separated for a month, for refusing a reconciliation. The jury had accepted the defence's argument that he had felt 'dishonoured' by the separation, and the appellate court upheld the decision on the basis that the fact they were no longer a couple did not negate his feeling of humiliation, and that, in any case, the 'victim's behaviour was not exactly shy and retiring'.[20]

Although one operative principle in the Brazilian legal system is that the decision of the jury is sovereign, and cannot be challenged simply because the defence or prosecution disagree, a re-trial can be ordered when a jury verdict completely flies in the face of the evidence presented. Thus, some cases end up in the appellate courts, which have increasingly upheld the STJ's 1991 landmark ruling and struck down acquittals based on the 'honour defence', showing the gradual shift in judicial attitudes. A 2006 study carried out by feminist legal scholars examined 55 acquittals of spousal murder in the context of adultery considered in appellate courts between 1998 and 2003 (Pimentel et al., 2006, p. 112). In some cases, the courts allowed that a man is justified in using violence to 'protect his moral integrity, his family and his marriage'. The social norms and cultural arguments were also deployed. In one judge's view, 'It is all very well to say that a person whose honour is injured is the cheating partner… but that does not reflect reality, especially amongst us Latinos' (Pimentel et al., 2006, p. 99). However, the 1991 ruling had clearly stated that 'popular belief' was something entirely separate from the letter of the law. In some cases, the validity of the 'honour defence' was accepted by the courts, but other mitigating elements of Article 25 of the criminal code were deemed not to have been met, such as the 'reasonableness' of the force, or the 'imminence' of the threat represented (by the victim's behaviour). Murder was also considered to be an excessive emotional response to adultery. In cases where the acquittal was annulled and a re-trial ordered, the decisions were largely based on the 1991 ruling, demonstrating the importance of leadership in the judiciary through the vertical influence of precedential jurisprudence.

But completely eradicating the 'honour defence' has been a gradual and uneven process. In large part it depends on state-level judicial leaders indicating very clearly that it will not be entertained in court. Raoni Parreira, a prosecutor in the special unit handling feminicide cases in the Federal District, estimated that in the 30 or so cases he had worked on since 2015, only one defence lawyer had overtly attempted the honour defence.[21] However, he also noted how often the 'unfair provocation and violent emotion' argument was still being deployed as a back-door to the same rationale.[22] At a national level, the STJ has had to reiterate its position. In 2019, one the STJ justices, Rogério Schietti Cruz, ruled on an appeal put forward by a man who had strangled his female partner for talking to another man at a party. The accused had been convicted of homicide with four aggravating features (feminicide, asphyxia, senseless motive, and attacking a defenceless victim). His lawyers argued that the charge should be downgraded to *homicídio privilegiado* because he had acted under the influence of 'violent emotion' in response to the victim behaving 'abhorrently' and 'provocatively', driving him to 'primitive acts'. The comments made by the justice, a former prosecutor, were weary and dismissive in equal measure,

> *Although you can of course offer any defence arguments you want in court, I am rather surprised that in 2019 you are asking for the acquittal of a man who took his partner's life because she had supposedly damaged his honour. In a country that recorded 1,206 victims of feminicide in 2018 this sounds anachronistic at the very least.[23]*

Getting consistent justice for victims of feminicide still faces two structural obstacles. First, as long as the language of 'unfair provocation and violent emotion' is not excised from the criminal code, as recommended by the UNSR and the regional experts (MESECVI, 2012, p. 97; UN, 2016, para. 82(b), then Brazilian law continues to allow the paradox of a 'mitigated–aggravated homicide' where the mitigation consists, essentially, of blaming the victim. Second, Brazil's jury system produces perverse verdicts and acquittals based on defence team arguments that the STJ has repeatedly ruled to be irrelevant and inapplicable. The principle that the jury's decision is sovereign is still regarded by some jurists as equal, or superior, in weight to the countervailing principle that the verdict should be justifiable in terms of the evidence presented. There was dismay in September 2020 when a majority on the first panel of the STF upheld the acquittal of a man who had stabbed to death his ex-wife, enraged because he thought she was having an affair. Minas Gerais TJ and the STJ both appealed on the grounds that the 'honour' defence used by his lawyers has been ruled inadmissible. This STF ruling contradicted the STJ's 1991 ruling. On 26 February 2021, in response to public outcry and a legal petition, one of the STF justices, Dias Toffoli, issued a unilateral ruling that the 'honour defence' was inadmissible, as an 'odious, inhuman and cruel' argument that blamed the victim for her own injury or death. This position will likely be ratified by the full court.

GETTING TO TRIAL AND IMPROVING CONVICTION RATES

Until recently women in Brazil have had greater trust in the police than in the judiciary in relation to gender-based violence. As an institution, the police constitute a frontline, responding immediately to protect a victim, arrest an aggressor, or investigate a feminicide. The courts have been more distant, particularly when it comes to prosecuting criminal cases, even though the Maria da Penha law accelerated immensely the process of getting judicial restraining orders granted to protect women at risk.

This lack of faith in the judiciary has been slow to shift. A 2006 survey showed that 71% of female respondents agreed that 'Brazilian courts treats violence against women as unimportant'. Barely half of the respondents agreed that 'Brazilian courts punish perpetrators in cases of domestic violence', a figure that rose to only 60% for cases of feminicide (Instituto Patrícia Galvão, 2006, p. 5). The survey was repeated in 2013 and, whilst there was almost universally some familiarity with the Maria da Penha law, scepticism persisted about official responses. Some 75% of respondents felt that violence against women in general, and by intimate partners, was never or rarely punished. Even in the case of feminicide this distrust stood at 67% (Instituto Patrícia Galvão, 2013, p. 47). Although 57% of respondents felt that feminicides were being punished somewhat or a lot more severely than before, 85% also felt that men who murdered women were still getting off lightly. This 'justice gap' was attributed to the slowness of the justice system (42%), low sentences (29%), lack of priority given to such cases (14%), and incompetence (13%) (Instituto Patrícia Galvão, 2013, pp. 48–50).

Since 2006, the national bodies of the three judicial branches had been setting up specialist units, improving data gathering, trained legal operators, and developed national policies on gender-based violence. The CNJ and CNMP had also been consulted on the feminicide law, and this accumulated capacity and engagement enabled these bodies, post-2015, to pursue better analysis of the underlying patterns of feminicide, develop inter-agency collaboration, produce training packages and guidelines for prosecuting and trying feminicide, and undertake periodic efforts to clear the backlog of pending cases in line with the National Guidelines. By designating feminicide as aggravated homicide, the feminicide law raised the available prison sentences and allowed alleged perpetrators to be treated with greater severity and restrictions. It also galvanised judicial institutions to take targeted action to accelerate the process of getting to trial and raise the conviction rate in feminicide cases.

Prosecuting more Effectively

The prosecutor's office actively embraced the cause of prosecuting feminicide more effectively as part of its national strategy on justice and public security. The national governing body produced its own manual (CNMP, 2019), and a number of states developed their own intra- and inter-agency guidelines for handling feminicide prosecutions. The manual instructs prosecutors how to oversee the police investigation to ensure proper crime scene preservation, forensics, and chain of custody of evidence.[24] Charges can be brought even before the police investigation is concluded, in order to speed things up. The CNMP's own permanent committee on domestic violence issued two statements confirming that feminicide has an 'objective' character, that is, it is rooted in 'historical and cultural power inequalities' (CNMP, 2019, p. 28). This view is reflected in the emphasis that prosecutors, in their concluding arguments, give to structural drivers of feminicide, whilst judges are more likely to focus on the individual characteristics of the offender, for example, whether he was drunk or is generally aggressive (Machado, 2015). This approach is also reminiscent of the efforts of prosecutors in the early twentieth century to characterise those who killed 'for reasons of passion' as in fact cold, calculating, vicious, and brutish (Borelli, 2005). Prosecutors are advised to add one or more charges of 'base motive', if the killing was preceded by an argument, and to insist that 'violent emotion' and 'provocation' are put, in that order, in two separate *quesitos* so that jurors can see that perpetrators often act in rage and anger in the absence of any objective trigger. This approach, combined with improved police investigations on which the prosecutors can rest their arguments, is leading to higher conviction rates and quicker processing in feminicide cases. The prosecutor's office in the Federal District reported in March 2020 that it had brought feminicide charges in 68 cases between March 2015 and November 2019. Of those 40 were concluded, with 39 convictions, and an average sentence of 21 years.[25] The juries rejected the aggravating element of feminicide in only two cases. All cases of feminicides committed prior to December 2017 had been tried, whilst 19 more were at the preliminary hearing stage.

Speeding up Proceedings

One of the CNJ's priorities was to speed up the wheels of justice. Many of the key recommendations of the IACHR's 2001 report on the Maria da Penha case concerned improving judicial proceedings and processes. Paragraph 61 noted, *inter alia*, the need to

> conduct a serious, impartial, and exhaustive investigation to determine responsibility for the irregularities or unwarranted delays that prevented rapid and effective prosecution of the perpetrator, and implement the appropriate administrative, legislative, and judicial measures.

The National Guidelines also stress that legal process should be conducted in a timely manner.

The CNJ decided to focus efforts over a concentrated time period to tackle the backlog of outstanding cases. In 2014, it promoted National Jury Trial Week across the country. In 2016, this turned into National Jury Trial Month, held in November each year, as it became evident that a week was not long enough. The CNJ asked the state judiciaries to prioritise certain types of cases such as those involving murders of women, minors, or police officers, murders by police, murders in bars and nightclubs, and cases where the perpetrator was on remand. Some of the feminicide cases tried in this concerted push included historic ones. In November 2016, a court in Pernambuco convicted Paulo Roberto Pereira da Silva, in absentia, of shooting dead 16-year-old Maria Auxiliadora de Menezes Gomes, 28 years earlier, for breaking off their engagement. Although the accused remained at large, the prosecution wanted to make it clear that feminicide would no longer go unpunished, under any circumstance.

The backlog is gradually being cleared. In 2017, 285,261 cases were awaiting trial, of which 54,916 had had the indictment confirmed at an evidentiary hearing. The number of pending cases was reduced in 2018 to 185,898, with 43,199 cases ready for trial. November 2018 saw 3,531 trials completed, of which 268 were feminicide cases. The conviction rate for the latter is note-worthy, running at an average of 64% over the five years of this programme, and rising year on year. In 2018, it was 87%, much higher than the rate for killings of children or of police officers (CNJ, 2019a, pp. 15, 17). In 2019, there was a further 6% increase in cases slated to go to trial and a 7% increase in those that actually did (84%).[26] The conviction rate of 90% reflects the efforts of police and prosecutors to provide a solid evidentiary base and of the judiciary to reduce the influence of specious exculpatory strategies (CNJ, 2020). It also reflects changing public attitudes to this crime and undermines the notion that local patriarchal attitudes will lead jurors to acquit.

A number of states have also adopted protocols to tackle delays in the justice system. These are intended to ensure that all the agencies of the criminal justice system follow the same set of principles, even if they have different roles in the process. Some courts fast-track domestic violence and feminicide cases: the TJ in Rio de Janeiro instituted the Violet-Orange Protocol, pledging that all requests to the courts for urgent protection measures would be processed within four hours if the woman's life was at risk, and support and protection be provided swiftly to survivors and indirect victims of feminicide. In others, prosecutors and courts mark feminicide cases with a coloured label so that they get fast-tracked. Courts also worked on removing the blockages that create the exces-sive *tempo de gaveta*. For example, Paraná's TJ collaborated with counterparts in neighbouring jurisdictions to get perpetrators arrested across state borders. Such efforts should begin to bring down the average time to trial to under a year.

Close analysis of the way that feminicide cases proceed through the courts also suggests that judges need continuing training to understand the dimensions of feminicide. It is evident that some judges, like some police and prosecutors, understand feminicide purely as a crime of domestic violence, which is only half of its legal definition. In a case in Piauí, where a woman had been murdered and her body hidden in the killer's freezer, before being dumped on waste-ground, one of the *quesitos* asked if there was any prior intimate relationship between victim and killer. As there was not, the charge of feminicide was removed.[27]

In conclusion, the Brazilian justice system has significantly improved the effectiveness with which it handles feminicide cases, although the wording of the criminal code and conduct of jury trials still leaves worrying loopholes. Justice is still slow, but efforts are being made to expedite feminicide cases. However, national judicial authorities have not yet met the UNSR's recom-mendation that systematic analysis of feminicide cases should include data on the prosecution and punishment of perpetrators. This is particularly impor-tant for attempted feminicide cases, on which there is less data, and yet where there is a survivor who requires further assistance to avoid future violence. Thus, prevention and protection strategies are the subject of Chapter Five.

NOTES

1. For a full list of the legal strategies they employed, and the court decisions on them, see https://www.jusbrasil.com.br/topicos/101683525/paulo-eduardo-costa-steinbach.

2. https://www.mpsc.mp.br/noticias/mpsc-recorre-de-resultado-de-juri-de-reu-que-matou-esposa-atropelada?print=sim.

3. This tendency was visible in my analysis of the 85 cases of feminicide committed in Pernambuco in 2018 in the #UmaPorUma database. There are, however, cases where the opposite has occurred.

4. This is derived from my analysis of cases in the #UmaPorUma database, and also the data available on the TJ site in Santa Catarina. There are no national data.

5. According to Pierpaolo Cruz Bottini, a University of São Paulo law professor and a former head of the Secretariat for Reform of the Judiciary in the Ministry of Justice. http://g1.globo.com/brasil/noticia/2013/09/por-que-a-justica-brasileira-e-tao-lenta.html.

6. For more details on her story, see the website of the institute she set up http://www.institutomariadapenha.org.br/quem-e-maria-da-penha.html, her autobiography (Penha, 1994), and the details in the IACHR (2001) report.

7. The STF is an unusual hybrid, in global terms, in combining two apparently counterposed forms of constitutional review, concentrated and diffuse.

8. https://www.jota.info/stf/do-supremo/pgr-pede-ao-stf-execucao-imediata-de-pena-em-feminicidio-de-1999-03052019.

9. The other crimes are racism and involvement in armed groups that threaten the democratic order.

10. Details of the bill's progress through the Congress can be found at https://www25.senado.leg.br/web/atividade/materias/-/materia/136775.

11. The other crimes that go to a jury trial are homicide, incitement to suicide, infanticide, and abortion.

12. Anthropologist Roberto Kant de Lima pioneered the study of the philosophical and cultural history and peculiarities of jury trials in Brazil. See Lima (2010) and Schritzmeyer (2013).

13. For discussion of ideal type *quesitos* for a feminicide trial see Pires (2015).

14. '*praticado sob um estado de total perturbação dos sentidos e da inteligência*', Article 27, para. 4 of the 1890 Criminal Code.

15. This is distinct from mental retardation, mental illness, or inability to understand the criminality of an act.

16. The jurors rejected the other possibilities that the victim had caused her own death, or that she had suffered bodily injury followed by death.

17. https://catarinas.info/justica-ameniza-pena-para-autor-do-feminicidio-de-yara-steinbach/.

18. http://www.oabsp.org.br/sobre-oabsp/grandes-causas/o-caso-doca-street.

19. Recurso Especial 1.517/PR, 6 a. T., j. 11.03.1991, DJU 15.04.1991, p. 4309.

20. REsp 203632/MS, 6ª T, j. 19.04.2001, DJ 19.12.2002, p. 454.

21. In an interview with Metrópoles 'De defesa da honra a forte emoção: os argumentos dos feminicidas', 5 May 2019. https://www.youtube.com/watch?time_continue=3&v=cIgy4-BAbuM&feature=emb_logo.

22. This was also noted in a survey of feminicide cases in Piauí (Villa, 2020).

23. https://www.conjur.com.br/2019-nov-12/schietti-cruz-repudia-tese-defesa-honra-feminicidio.

24. In Brazil, the prosecutor's office has a routine oversight function in relation to the investigative police.

25. One accused was found mentally incompetent.

26. The conviction rate for police accused of homicide was just 34%, and of individual accused of murdered an officer 50%. The other priority cases sent to trial in 2019 were stalled cases in which charges had been brought prior to 2015 but not reached trial.

27. Information from Eugênia Villa.

Chapter Five

PREVENTING FEMINICIDE

INTRODUCTION

'Feminicide is easy to investigate, but hard to prevent', Brazilian police officers often say. The first part has proven to be true because, generally, the perpetrators were known to the victim and clear-up rates are high. Yet, in Brazil, as elsewhere, most cases of domestic violence do not escalate to murder, and 80% of women killed by intimate partners have had no prior contact with the police. It was perplexing that, despite the apparent success of the 2006 Maria da Penha law, which had encouraged more women to report domestic violence, the number of women being murdered continued to rise steadily, from 3,778 in 2007 to 4,836 in 2014. The 2015 law was spurred by this concern. But, as the Brazilian congresswoman reviewing the feminicide bill noted in her committee report, 'criminal law is not about prevention'. Although feminicide is often pre-meditated, many perpetrators commit suicide or give themselves up to the authorities, indifferent to the deterrent threat of arrest or punishment.

Prevention of feminicide requires multiple strategies from a range of actors. The section of the Maria da Penha law dedicated to prevention (Article 8) sets out specific responsibilities for the police. It also underscores the need for a co-ordinated multi-agency approach, promoting the vertical integration of the initiatives of federal, state level, and municipal governments, and the horizontal integration of the different agencies of the criminal justice system with the policy actors in public security, social welfare, health, education, housing and employment, and with NGOs. The prevention strategies also emphasise awareness raising about domestic violence through the media and in educational settings.

This chapter examines how the three levels of prevention – tertiary, secondary, and primary – have been developed in Brazil by a variety of governmental and non-governmental actors (Pasinato, Machado, & Ávila, 2019).

Prevention is focussed almost exclusively on intimate partner or family-related feminicide. Tertiary prevention occurs once a first incident has occurred, with post hoc intervention designed to deter both re-offending and re-victimisation. The chapter traces how local police forces have devised innovative tertiary prevention strategies and technologies to monitor and protect high-risk domestic violence victims and to deter aggressors. The next section examines the secondary prevention risk assessment tools developed by different actors in the criminal justice system to identify proximate factors indicating which individuals were more likely to commit, or be victims of, feminicide. The final section on primary prevention looks at actions aimed at addressing the underlying, structural drivers of gender-based violence, such as social attitudes towards women and how they are expressed in popular discourse, in law, and within social institutions, including criminal justice bodies.

ENFORCING RESTRAINING ORDERS

The Maria da Penha Patrols

In recent years, one of the most original police responses to the problem of the repetitive, cyclical, and often escalating characteristics of domestic abuse has been the establishment of the Maria da Penha police patrols (*Patrulhas/Rondas Maria da Penha*, hereafter patrols).[1] These specially trained and dedicated police teams focus on enforcing court-issued urgent protection measures (*medidas protetivas urgentes* – MPUs), which typically include stay-away orders. Before the advent of the patrols there was little monitoring and uneven sanctioning of breaches. One of the first systematic surveys, examining MPUs granted in the Federal District between 2006 and 2012, found that restraining orders were breached in 12% of cases, with no system established for following up with victims, or recording their reports of violations (Diniz & Gumieri, 2016, p. 219). Although confidence in the police had been rising steadily since the Maria da Penha law, victims knew that a piece of paper would not prevent retributive assault. In too many cases, women died with the injunction in their pocket, and this dissuaded victims from applying for them. Women are often skilled managers of dangerous individuals and have strategies for remaining safe. If reporting to the police disrupts that equilibrium, then they need reliable assurance that they will receive effective protection (Monckton Smith, Williams, & Mullane, 2014).

The patrols were set up by state-level military police forces, and some municipal guards, both of which have a primarily preventive remit and generally act as *first* responders, responding to emergency calls. Until 2006, both were completely marginal to the state's response to domestic violence, whose centre of gravity had been the DEAMs and the civil police since the mid-1980s. The Maria da Penha law restored responsibility to the first responder police, making explicit their *protective* remit. Articles 10 and 11 specified that the police should: immediately assist a victim who has been, or is about to be, assaulted; transport her to a hospital, a safe place, or a police station; and escort her to retrieve her belongings from home, if necessary. The law was also more directive about police action. Prior to 2006, without a specific law on domestic violence and only the generic statutory definitions of assault to guide them, police officers used their discretion. Some logged incidents as 'not a crime' (in police jargon, *desinteligência*) or as 'disputes' (*vias de fato*), some sent women back to their husbands and told them to put up with it, some tried to mediate between the couple, and some would 'teach the husband a lesson'. These strategies did not interrupt the cycle of violence very successfully (Meneghel et al., 2011). Post-2006, if there is evidence of bodily harm, then the attending officers must arrest the perpetrator and report the crime to a *delegacia*. Any civil police station chief, prosecutor, or the victim can then request a local judge to impose MPUs. The ones imposed on the perpetrator under Article 22 of the Maria da Penha law are designed to reduce the likelihood of further assault, and include: the suspension of the right to own or carry a firearm; eviction from the shared residence; and restrictions on approaching the victim, her family, witnesses, or children. The court can also impose measures additional to those outlined in the law. It was these legal changes, in combination with women's movement concern to support victims, that prompted local police forces to develop a specialised and systematic *second* line of police response to domestic violence and feminicide prevention.

The origins of the patrols lie in the late 1990s, when women's organisations were focussed on providing post hoc services to victims (shelters, referral centres, and counselling services; Barsted, 2011, p. 19). In 1997, the gender studies unit at the federal university and women's groups in the city of Uberlândia, in Minas Gerais, had set up *SOS Mulher e Família* (SOS Women and Families). This NGO ran the Women's Rights and Gender Policy Division in the city hall and opened a women's shelter. In 2003, moving to a more preventive approach, it established the Multidisciplinary Support Patrol (*Patrulha de Atendimento Multidisciplinar*), a programme run in partnership with the university, the city council, and the local military police unit. The latter assisted them logistically in their home visits to domestic violence victims, to whom they offered the services of volunteer social workers, lawyers, and psychologists.[2] A couple of years later, a senior military police officer, Lieutenant Colonel Cícero Nunes Moreira, was looking for effective intervention responses, having observed that 30% of all police callouts in his area of command related to domestic violence, often from just a few addresses.

As part of his continuing professional development, he had studied strategic planning, evidence-led violence reduction policies, crime concentration analysis, and community-oriented policing.[3] His Master's level thesis on repeat victimisation led him to scrutinise local domestic violence data as an exemplar of 'hot spots' (spatial locations where crimes are concentrated) and 'hot dots' (individuals who are subject to repeat victimisation) (Moreira, 2006). This 'pracademic' approach would inform the programme he later developed. On reviewing the Uberlândia initiative, he decided the police should play a greater role. In 2007, when he took command of the 34th Battalion in the state capital, Belo Horizonte, he set up as a pilot project the Domestic Violence Prevention Service, of which police patrols (*Patrulhas de Prevenção à Violência Doméstica* – PPVD) were the key element. He started testing new second response protocols, inspired by procedures used by English police forces in Leeds and Liverpool that he discovered during his studies. The new Patrols consisted of a pair of specially trained officers, generally one male and one female, in a clearly branded police car, that would carry out a series of visits to victims who had an MPU, enrol the couple in the programme, inform the victim of her rights under the Maria da Penha law, introduce her to the support agencies in the local protection network, and conduct a risk assessment and, later, a case review (Pereira & Ferreira, 2017). The aim was to empower the victim to make active choices in order to change her situation. They would also meet separately with the perpetrator to explain that he had committed a crime and, that if he re-offended, he would be arrested. This is essentially the procedure adopted by all subsequent Patrols in Brazil.

In 2010, Moreira was appointed commander for the whole city, enabling him to extend the prevention service to 8 battalions, 24 companies, and 48 specialist teams. The military police General Command mainstreamed the patrols by listing them as one of the military police's core services. Slowly the patrols expanded, operating in 23 municipalities by 2017, and 50 by mid-2020. From the outset, the frontline first responder officers were also put through a week of classroom training on how to understand gender power relations, 'read' the crime scene, interview effectively, and write a detailed and relevant police report that would assist the court in risk assessment. Domestic violence now forms part of basic training for all new recruits and prevention is considered an essential policing function by the force.

Meanwhile, in Rio Grande do Sul, similar challenges faced another police policy entrepreneur, Lieutenant Colonel Nádia Gerhard, who, in 2007, was the first woman to be given command of a battalion in the state. In her patch, covering several municipalities in a rural area, she also decided to prioritise enforcement of MPUs and in 2011 set up 'Operation Peaceful Family'.

As in Minas Gerais, this involved the military police checking in on abuse victims and filing reports about their safety. In 2012, after giving a talk at an international seminar on women and public security, sponsored by the state government agencies for women's rights and for policing, she was invited by the state governor to take up command of the 19th Battalion and roll out this project in the capital city, Porto Alegre. She set up the Maria da Penha patrols (the name by which these units are now most commonly known around Brazil) in four 'Peace Territories', neighbourhoods targeted for violence reduction and community policing interventions (Grossi & Spaniol, 2019, p. 300). Like Moreira, she also took an academic approach to her policing practice. In the dissertation for her professional Master's qualification in public security management at the local university, she carried out an analysis of the patrols' impact. Her survey of 147 victims enrolled in the programme revealed that 88% of respondents did not feel safe with just the MPU before the patrols started their visits, 86% reported that the aggressor was now respecting the restrained order, and 83% had not needed to ring the police to report a further incident (Gerhard, 2014, pp. 155–159). Here the expansion of the programme was also halting, reaching 26 more cities between 2014 and 2017 (Grossi & Spaniol, 2019, p. 310), slowing after she left the police in 2016 to take up a career in politics, with an increase to 84 cities announced 2020. However, their impact was much wider than those in Minas Gerais. Gerhard was the first key diffuser of this new police practice as she hosted, and travelled to talk to, interested military police officers in other states (Grossi & Spaniol, 2019, p. 311).

One of the officers who visited Porto Alegre, in 2013, was Major Denice Santiago of the military police in Bahia, who became the public face of the patrols on Gerhard's retirement. Like her, she was a member of the first intake of female recruits into the military police in her state.[4] It took her two years to get the *Ronda Maria da Penha* set up, and she succeeded only with the backing of the local women's movement, given the rather half-hearted support from her own institution. Her colleagues held plenty of prejudices, seeing the patrol as a first, not second, response unit, as a waste of police resources, as a chance for male officers to have sexual relations with the victims, and as a unit for the work-shy.[5] In Rio Grande do Sul, Lt Col Gerhard dealt with the view that policing domestic violence was easy and not 'real' police work by training the officers of the force's elite armed response team (*Batalhão de Operações Especiais*) who deal with situations such as hostage taking. She impressed on them the much higher level of risk and unpredictability in domestic violence situations where emotions are running high and the perpetrator has nothing to negotiate, if his plan is feminicide–suicide.

The horizontal policy transfer of the patrols across Brazil is largely attributable to the influence of these two women officers, depending on which police forces visited them or had them come to give talks and training. The Bahia patrol had a somewhat greater multiplier force in the North and North-East, and the Rio Grande do Sul one in the South, South-East, and Centre-West. Both were acutely aware of the need to build high-level and multi-agency support for the patrols from the outset in order to get them institutionalised as quickly as possible. Gerhard had made a point of meeting the top decision-makers in each state she visited.[6] She also talked to national associations of judges, prosecutors, and public defenders, who became key local multipliers across the country, as judicial actors have an interest in ensuring that orders issued by the Domestic and Family Violence courts are complied with. The domestic violence units (CEVIDs) set up in every state appellate court have worked with police, particularly the municipal guards, to set up new patrols, as the judiciary has begun to compensate for the policy vacuum left in national government with the dismantling of the SPM. Whilst the national secretariat for policies on women (SPM) held ministerial status under the PT governments, it funded equipment for some of the early initiatives. In late 2017, the national Secretariat for Public Security (SENASP) began running a National Maria da Penha training course, in different locations, as part of a project to make the PMPs a nation-wide policy and promote common understandings and approaches. After 2018, there was little federal government promotion of the patrols.

There are no reliable and centrally collated figures as to how many patrols currently operate. My estimate, using available state-level data, is that there were around 300 patrols functioning by mid-2020 across Brazil. Some military police forces (such as Minas Gerais, Rio Grande do Sul, Federal District, and Paraíba) have established them right across the territory, whilst they are incipient in others, where there may be only one in the capital city. In states such as São Paulo, where the military police have shown no interest, municipal and judicial authorities have set up municipal patrols, and in some cases municipal police and military police patrols co-exist, potentially creating co-ordination problems and institutional conflicts. The Maria da Penha law does not specify *which* police force should protect victims of domestic violence, and this has led to a degree of functional overlap.

Inevitably with such a patchwork of initiatives, there is a variety of practice and local partnerships. For example, in São Paulo city, the municipal guard was asked to set up a Maria da Penha patrol by the state prosecutor's office. The latter triaged the cases that were then passed on, in 'red files', to the Guard to follow up. In other locations, the highest risk cases are selected by the DEAMs or by the Family and Domestic Violence courts. Information sharing is also a problem when different parts of the criminal justice system operate separate databases. The military police have to request access to the civil police and court files so that they can check background crime reports, the criminal records of perpetrators, and the details of MPUs. The municipal guards are not part of the state government law enforcement system, so have no access at all to the relevant databases.[7] The procedure by which police protection is activated also varies. Generally, the patrols wait to be notified of the highest risk cases, but in some the police visit the victim as soon as the request for an MPU is submitted, as it can take up to four days for the order to be granted, during which time the victim may feel extremely vulnerable.[8] Victims are also now being advised electronically about the result of their request, where previously they had to go in person to the court house. This was not easy for low-income women living far from the city centre.

Interviews with patrol co-ordinators across the country indicated how aware they are of their strategic role, and that it is only as part of a joined-up network that the patrols have proven to be effective 'interruptors' in the cycle of violence, deterring either a repetition or intensification of domestic violence. Major Santiago provided the other police forces that she and her colleagues trained and advised with their model Technical Co-operation Agreement, which sets out the distinct and inter-locking responsibilities of the various criminal justice system agencies and of local government. In September 2019, she hosted a meeting of patrols from nearby states in order to encourage the harmonisation of basic operating procedures, such as initial risk assessment, data collection, and reporting on the victim's status. As these patrols became institutionalised, they worked even more closely with the civil police, the DEAMs, the judiciary, and local statutory and civil society protection networks.

Their impacts have been positive in several dimensions. Many report that no woman enrolled in their protection programme has been a victim of feminicide. The visits (scheduled and unscheduled) displace the authority of the abuser in the home, and the visibility of the specially marked police cars tells him that he is being monitored in public space. This signals to low-income, high-violence communities that the police are physically present in their neighbourhood concerned with inter-personal conflicts and citizen security, and as a result the patrols have boosted police legitimacy. The patrols are often attached to community-policing departments,[9] and their success has reinforced this approach within organisations still inclined to understand policing as a repressive activity involving the show and use of force.

Most importantly, the patrols encouraged more women to report abuse, at an earlier stage, and to seek protection. The patrols' experience, in addition to better training on gender-based violence, is shifting understanding within police institutions about how and when women choose to disclose abuse and seek help. The popular myth that women 'like to be beaten' (*gosta de apanhar*) is fading fast. When surveyed, women report a range of reasons for their reluctance, such as social shame, pressure from family and social networks (for example, their church), and economic dependence. They may also fear that the police will dismiss certain forms of abuse, such as verbal threats, that are actually key mechanisms of coercive control and effective in silencing victims. Therefore, victims need a high level of confidence that the police will not only take their reports of abuse seriously, but also act quickly and effectively to stop the perpetrators repeating or intensifying the abuse. This is particularly important for women who have been victims of attempted feminicide. In 2019, the civil police filed 17% more requests for urgent protection orders than in 2018 (FBSP, 2020a, p. 125), indicating that the system is responding to this need.

Panic and Protection Apps and GPS Tracking

Several police forces have embraced information and communication technologies, and produced their own apps, using GPS data and in-house expertise, to increase reporting and improve enforcement of MPUs. In Piauí, a state where the civil police took the lead in developing best practice on gender-based violence (Neme & Martins, 2018, pp. 25–26), their app, *Salva Maria*, had two functions. One acted as an emergency panic button that activated a first response by the military police. The other allowed anonymous reporting of domestic abuse to the civil police, thus functioning rather like the 180 hotline that operates nationally out of the Ministry for Women, Family, Women, and Human Rights.[10]

The first instruments used to enforce MPUs were 'panic button' devices that the victim could use to alert the police that the aggressor had breached the exclusion zone. In 2013, Espírito Santo state launched the first one. When activated, it sent a signal to the central municipal police dispatch, which also received details of the victim, the perpetrator, the MPUs in place, contacts for her friends and family and the address with Google street view (Tavares & Campos, 2018). The device would also automatically start recording any conversation in the immediate vicinity, which could be used as proof in any further criminal proceedings. This is a common feature in many of these schemes, and in some the police control room can monitor the conversation in real time, assisting the police response. A number of other police forces (mainly municipal guards) followed suit with similar schemes, although the alarm devices are now being replaced by smartphone apps. In Belém do Pará, a high-risk victim can receive a smartphone with the app installed. If she feels unsafe, she presses it three times and a black screen appears so that the assailant cannot see the app. It vibrates a set number of times to let her know her call is being monitored and help is on its way, in the form of one of the 12 motor-bike patrols with specially trained officers (*Ronda Ostensiva Municipal*). The monitoring is kept open for 30 minutes to give time for officers to reach her.

In the earlier versions of these apps, the tracking was more basic. Often 'stay-away' orders specify restricted locations, most typically the victim's residence. However, as the alarm devices and phone apps are now able to send GPS data to the police, the police dispatchers can protect the victim wherever she is. Whilst the onus initially was on the victim to alert the police, increasingly the police can keep track of the offender using electronic tagging, which courts can mandate when issuing an MPU. A bill currently under consideration in the Senate would alter the text of the Maria da Penha law to make it obligatory for anyone subject to a removal or stay-away order to wear an electronic tag.

For institutional reasons, the municipal guards are more inclined to issue women with alarms or apps that they have to activate, whilst the military police prefer to monitor the movements of perpetrators. Electronic tagging of prisoners (both on remand and on parole) has been regulated in Brazil since 2011 and is widely used. As the state government prison system already possesses the ankle tags, a 24-hour monitoring service, and an integrated information system linked into the courts and police databases, it was easy for the state-level law enforcement agencies to piggyback on these and extend their use to high-risk domestic abusers. For example, under Ceará state's *Mulher sem Medo* (Women without Fear) programme, a joint initiative of the state judiciary, public prosecutor's office, and public defender's office, launched in 2014, the protected woman is alerted by an SMS and an alarm that vibrates and blinks if the perpetrator comes within a certain radius. The monitoring centre will also call her.[11]

The use of GPS monitoring has many advantages. It protects the victim wherever she is. As noted earlier, many feminicides are often committed after months of stalking and planning and occur in public places. The patrols may miss her when they visit the residence, if she is at work or has opted to move out of her home. Neither the victim nor the patrols can be alert 24/7 but an electronic monitoring system can, and it removes the onus of self-protection from the victim. It also gives her more warning to escape a potentially deadly situation.

GPS monitoring also benefits perpetrators by preventing the perpetrator inadvertently coming too close (many systems alert the wearer via a speaker on the tag). Law 13.641, passed in 2018, made it a crime to violate any court-imposed injunction. Although the penalty (three months to two years in prison) is low, and would automatically be converted into a non-custodial disposition under Brazilian law, a conviction creates a criminal record and, in the case of future assaults, the perpetrator would no longer be able to benefit from being a first-time offender (which affects pre-trial detention and the length of the sentence). This change in the law, in conjunction with Article 20 of the Maria da Penha law, which allows a judge to issue a preventive detention order against dangerous individuals, has led, in some places, to more perpetrators being arrested by the Maria da Penha patrols and their first response colleagues. Amendments to the Maria da Penha law supported by the Bolsonaro administration have tended to increase prison sentences and promote the use of preventive detention. However, the Brazilian prison system is grossly overcrowded, dominated by gangs, and steeped in a culture of aggressive hyper-masculinity, which is hardly conducive to reducing re-offending by domestic abusers. GPS monitoring and electronic tagging, where used, has resulted in a drop in breaches of stay-away orders. They enable offenders to stay out of the prison system and attend the therapy/discussion groups often mandated by judges, which are far more effective at prevention. US studies of the impact of GPS monitoring suggest that both victims and aggressors are better able to get on with their lives, with the latter appreciating that the monitoring actually protects them from any false accusations.

The Maria da Penha patrols and GPS monitoring are complementary technologies, not alternatives, as they perform different functions. So, when the state of Pernambuco launched its Justice for Women programme in 2013, it initiated both at the same time. The use of both highlights the need for the specialist second response patrols to work closely with their colleagues in the first response patrols, which will generally be the ones to respond to an alert about a breach.[12] Although they will have data about the victim and her MPUs, they also need to be trained in how to handle a potentially volatile domestic violence situation, and assess the risk.

RISK ASSESSMENT TOOLS

Risk assessment is a key element of secondary prevention. A triage process should identify who is at highest risk of mounting violence in order to assign them to the protection of a Maria da Penha patrol and/or into an electronic tagging and tracing programme. But who should do the assessment and what tools are effective in predicting the relatively rare, but catastrophic, outcome of feminicide? Domestic violence escalates in complex ways, and does not follow a straightforward linear path that starts with verbal and psychological abuse, intensifies into physical violence and threats, and culminate in murder.

Qualitative analysis of feminicide cases conducted by police forces, prosecutor's office, and NGOs shows that intermediary stages involving incremental use of violence may be absent, which is why the verbal threats that women report should be taken seriously. They now have a better understanding of the role played by contextual factors in the relationship, the home, and the perpetrator's own triggers and stressors.[13] International research has identified important 'risk markers' indicating potential escalation to feminicide. These include objective elements, such as the presence of firearms or alcohol, but it seems that subjective elements are more indicative. These include suicidal ideation on the part of the abuser, their use of strangulation in previous assaults (Sherman, Strang, & O'Connor, 2017), specific thought patterns of trauma-based entitlement, humiliated fury, insecurity, and toxic shame (Hill, 2019), and shifts in the abuser's behaviour, such as increased stalking, a shift to 'last chance thinking', and active planning of homicide and suicide (Monckton Smith, 2019).

The very first domestic violence patrols assessed risk by drawing on their experience and the criminological methodologies the officers had studied. However, once they began working systematically in partnership, it became clear that the other criminal justice agencies were also using their own assessment tools, which the National Council of the Prosecutor's office (CNMP) has tried to systematise. Its national public security and justice strategy included a goal to respond faster to feminicide cases and to reduce overall incidence, which led CNMP's lead advisor on the issue to speak at a UN event about their initiatives. There he met the European Union's lead on gender issues,[14] and this led to an EU-supported partnership with academics from Brazil, led by Wânia Pasinato, and academics from a Portuguese university, the Faculdade Nova de Lisboa.[15] A field trip to various European countries and a survey of risk assessment instruments from around the world, such as the DASH questionnaire for domestic abuse, stalking, and honour-based violence adopted in 2009 by the Chief Police officers in the United Kingdom, led to the creation of the FRIDA risk assessment form (*Formulário de Avaliação de Risco*).[16] It consists of 19 questions covering issues such as: the victim's previous experiences of assault or coercive control; recent escalation; evidence of other violence by the perpetrator (for example, against pets); 'flag' issues such as mental health problems (but not suicidal ideation), medication, alcohol or drug consumption and access to weapons; stressors such as financial difficulty and recent separation; and the vulnerability of the victim (pregnancy, very young, and dependent children). The yes/no answers to these questions are totted up and a summary box gives a final score, indicating low, medium, or high risk. There are also more open-ended, subjective questions to be filled in by the attending professional.

This was intended to replace the four or five different forms being used by prosecutors around the country, and to be an instrument shared with the judiciary, with which the CNMP had set up a working group. But the CNJ created their own, based on the FRIDA form,[17] containing 24 questions, with additional multiple-choice questions for more details. There were no subjective questions for the form filler or final numerical ranking of risk, as the CNJ regarded it as the judges' role to draw their own conclusions. Thus, for a whilst, the two justice agencies operated with parallel instruments, with the prosecutors using the CNMP's, and judges using the CNJ's. The CNMP's was envisaged as an instrument for use during the earliest contact with the victim to assist with referral, and thus it was adopted by the 180 national Domestic Violence Hotline, run by the Ministry for Women, Family, and Human Rights. Under a co-operation agreement, the Ministry sends the CNMP the data on the abusers and victims, the risk classification applied to the cases, and the details of subsequent referrals. This has helped the CNMP to track the effectiveness of the system's response to domestic violence reporting and also to build the long-overdue national database on gender-based violence. However, the police were more inclined to use the CNJ's version. A senior officer with the São Paulo civil police noted it was easier to follow and that the CNJ had allowed that it could be filled in by a police officer in the absence of a judge.[18] The police had also been lobbying to be given the power to issue the protection measures necessary to protect a victim at risk without having to wait up to four days for a judge to decide. This was granted by Law 13.827, passed in May 2019, which states, in order of preference, that a judge, local police *delegado*, or any police officer may remove the aggressor from the victim's home. A judge must be informed within 24 hours and decide whether to uphold the measure, and details of the case must be entered into the CNMP's database. In Brazil's highly judicialised system this is a concession to the civil police *delegados*, whose professional entry requirement is a law degree and who therefore see themselves as judicial actors as much as police professionals.

This institutional rivalry and duplication of effort was overcome finally, in March 2020, when the CNMP and CNJ signed a joint resolution approving a single, national FRIDA.[19] It is based on the 24 multi-layered questions used in the CNJ's form (now increased to 27) and adds in the CNMP's subjective questions. The format does not allow for any mechanical ranking of risk. It is intended for use by the civil police when the victim registers a complaint, or by judge or prosecutor, as part of the first response. It may also be used by other actors in the prevention, response, and support networks, given the key role they play.

PRIMARY PREVENTION

Primary prevention of gender-based violence is being carried out by a very wide range of actors in Brazilian society, including grassroots groups, NGOs, health and education services, and the criminal justice institutions themselves, which have not only intensified their training of staff but also engage in general awareness raising. As the first and second response services, police forces have now begun to address not just professional understanding and practice around domestic violence and feminicide, but also their incidence within their own ranks.

Changing Police Cultures

Changing the working culture of the police is one of the structural aspects of prevention. The workplace culture of Brazilian police institutions is very male dominated, particularly in the state military police forces, which all have either formal or informal upper limits on the percentage of female officers admitted to their ranks (Pivetta, 2020; SENASP, 2013).[20] Their militarised culture, training, operational norms, and hierarchy can create a toxic environment. Officers' reluctance to divulge personal worries can lead to bullying, sexual harassment, and inter-personal violence (FBSP, 2015). In the training sessions I held with police on gender-based violence, officers related how their institutions simply ignored cases of domestic violence committed by their own colleagues, often against fellow officers.

However, some police forces have put in place policies to tackle the inter-related problems of hyper-masculinity, mental health problems, and domestic abuse. It is now recognised that suicidal thoughts are a red flag for feminicide amongst law enforcement professionals, whose suicide rate (per 100,000 individuals) is three to four times higher than that in the general population (FBSP, 2019). A São Paulo study of deceased military police officers revealed the histories of 'Sávio', who abused his wife and 'would get aggressive when sent to incidents involving domestic rows', 'Miguel' who died of burns sustained whilst setting fire to his ex-wife's residence, 'João' who shot himself in the head after killing his wife, and 'Hilda', who was herself a victim of domestic violence (OPESP, 2019, p. 36). The drivers of police suicide are multi-causal – low salaries, the financial and health stress of moonlighting, post-traumatic stress from exposure to violent situations, and substance dependence. But the risk is compounded by easy access to firearms, which is the method of choice and a facilitating factor for over 80% of police suicides and police-committed feminicides, as officers take their service weapons home with them (OPESP, 2019, pp. 76–78). Denise Quioca's former partner had been sacked from the police just days before he shot her dead, carrying three service weapons that he had retained. Several police forces now have internal directives to ensure that officers accused of domestic abuse have their service weapons, and personal firearms, confiscated from them whilst under investigation.[21] Even President Bolsonaro, who had campaigned loudly for the liberalisation of the gun laws in Brazil, approved an October 2019 law that altered the Maria da Penha law to allow for the seizure of an abuser's firearm as part of a court-ordered protective measure.[22]

In the Federal District, academics and officers identified patterns of domestic abuse in the local police, which led to new intervention strategies. Analysis of the death certificates of 338 women who suffered violent intentional deaths between 2006 and 2011 showed that 96 were domestic violence feminicides. In 12 cases, the perpetrator committed suicide (Diniz, Costa, & Gumieri, 2015). Six of these involved members of the security services who were responsible for nine feminicides, meaning that the likelihood of a police officer committing suicide after a feminicide was five times higher than in the general population.[23] The head of training at the military police academy then carried out a unique survey of police misconduct investigations for her Master's dissertation (Cardoso, 2016). Of 264 internal disciplinary cases opened between 2012 and 2014 involving domestic assault, frequently as a result of a relationship ending, 95% resulted in no administrative punishment and 85% were closed for 'lack of proof' (Ibid., p. 71). The officers' victims were left unprotected, and the perpetrators received neither sanction nor appropriate support. She and the head of the internal affairs department discovered that domestic violence constituted the second most frequent reason for a disciplinary investigation to be opened, with 54 in 2018 alone (Schlittler, 2019, p. 120). With the support of the Women's Legal Unit (*Núcleo Judiciário da Mulher*) of the TJ, in 2017 they set up the Maria da Penha Instruction Programme, of which the key component was the Men's Therapeutic Discussion groups. Military police officers and firefighters charged with domestic violence offences are required to attend six sessions designed to help them understand the law, non-violent communication, and common beliefs about gender and violence, and take responsibility for their actions. Whilst such encounter groups for perpetrators have become widespread in Brazil (Beiras, Nascimento, & Incrocci, 2019), this was the first targeted at law enforcement personnel. In 2018, around 50 officers went through the programme and none had further complaints made against them or committed feminicide (Schlittler, 2019, p. 128).

In 2009, the Minas Gerais military police hospital, which treats police personnel and their families, set up a Committee on Domestic Violence to identify and support patients disclosing domestic violence (Brigagão, 2018).[24] The hospital trained its staff in questioning and listening techniques, then improved its protocols in how cases were treated and tracked. Victims are assisted in reporting the crime to the *delegacia*, the relevant battalion (to which the victim or the abuser is attached) is informed so that appropriate action can be taken (confiscation of firearm and internal disciplinary hearing), and the victim is referred to the local support network. Whilst there is undoubtedly still a high degree of under-reporting, the committee's work legitimates concern for domestic violence in the ranks. It also connects health services with policing, underscoring how domestic violence needs to be treated not just as a criminal problem but also as a public health issue.

The ingrained misogyny in police culture is beginning to crack. The increase of women, both in new intakes and senior positions, is starting to mitigate the association of policing with performative masculinity. A number of military police forces have set support systems for women within their ranks on issues including sexual harassment, bullying, and domestic violence. The first was the Maria Felipa Centre, set up by Major Denice Santiago in 2006 (Paredes, 2017).[25] The military police in the Federal District set up a gender office (*Escritório de Gênero*) in 2016, and a similar unit (*Núcleo Assistencial de Acompanhamento e Orientação*) was established in Maranhão in 2017, which undertook to educate the entire force on gender-based violence, not just as something 'out there', that they police on behalf of others, but as an internal problem (Bueno & Pacheco, 2020).

Training is key to improving police responses to gender-based violence, and it is encouraging that some forces now train not just their specialist units, but also all new recruits, on domestic violence and on the prevention and investigation of feminicide (Martins & Machado, 2020). Some of that training is purely internal, provided either through the police academies, or by specialist officers (in the patrols and DEAMs) training their non-specialist frontline colleagues. In Alagoas, the Maria da Penha patrols train other frontline officers, and certificate each battalion once its personnel have completed the programme. This is intended to ensure harmonised procedures across the force. In some places training is provided by the police's partners in the local protection network, with prosecutors, judges, and representatives of women's groups giving talks and workshops as part of basic training or continuing professional development.

That said, there is still a clear training gap. When I conducted workshops on gender-based violence for law enforcement officials in various locations around Brazil, as part of a project with the FBSP, it became evident how patchy police training was. In nearly all cases, the majority of participants, even those that worked in specialist units dedicated to domestic violence and feminicide, indicated in our pre-training survey that they had received little or no training on these issues. A typical training session on domestic violence might consist of a two-hour lecture on the law, often delivered by a non-specialist. This is what motivated the military police in the Federal District to get their programme, Police Intervention in Domestic Violence Incidents (*Intervenção Policial em Ocorrências de Violência Doméstica*) integrated into the basic training of new recruits. Good training can also alter police culture, not just through the content but also the teaching methods. Some forces already use more interactive teaching styles that are more effective than the passive lecture format. For example, the civil police academy in São Paulo uses role play to train DEAM officers across the state (Schlittler & Hanashiro, 2019). Thus, the manual that I and Juliana Martins produced with the FBSP encourages police trainers to use dynamic pedagogical methods that develop core attitudes, knowledge of the law, and a reflexive approach to practice. It also became clear in our training sessions that individual law enforcement agencies were often unsure how their responsibilities around gender-based violence dove-tailed with those of other agencies, so the manual also stresses the importance of inter-agency training and collaboration to strengthen local networks (FBSP, 2020b).

Community Education

Since 2006, criminal justice agencies and local NGOs have started working with perpetrators, who can be required to attend discussion groups as part of the conditions imposed on them by the court, as a form of secondary prevention. More unusual is a primary prevention project in Bahia, led by male military police officers, that engages men who are not yet perpetrators in communities with high reported levels of domestic violence (Bueno & Brigagão, 2018). Justice-sector actors are also engaging with schools and civil society organisations in local protection networks, raising awareness of their work and of the law. To an extent they are substituting for what the educational system should be providing. The Maria da Penha law directs that 'curricula, at all levels of education, should highlight content relating to human rights, equity in gender, ethnic and racial relations, and the problem of domestic and family violence' (Article 8, para. IX). But gender has become politicised and contentious. In 2014, the content of the National Education Plan was used by the religious right to attack the PT government. This was further fuelled by a one-man campaign, *Escola sem Partido* (literally, 'unbiased school'), that alleged that education at all levels had become contaminated with (left-wing) ideological indoctrination.

The pro-Bolsonaro state government of Santa Catarina backed attempts to remove the topic of gender relations from the primary school curriculum (Auras, 2020, p. 22), and dozens of bills were proposed in municipal legislatures around the country. However, to date such moves have been struck down as unconstitutional by the higher courts (Leão, 2019, pp. 63–67).

Education and awareness-raising work with the general public have also been carried out by a range of governmental and non-governmental bodies in Brazil. For example, Avon, the cosmetics company has 1.2 million sales representatives across Brazil, giving it a unique reach into diverse communities. The Avon Institute has supported awareness raising around gender-based violence since 2008, funding surveys into victimisation, men's attitudes, inter-generational transmission, and shifts in debates on social media. It has run annual conferences, promoted creative approaches to recognising domestic violence, and supported police training and excellence by identifying and rewarding good and innovative practices in the justice system (the FBSP's Stamp of Good Practice, awarded in three competitions in 2017, 2018, and 2019).[26] Major news organisations, such as Globo, have joined forces with local women's groups and national NGOs to document feminicide and publicise reports on the levels of gender-based violence, and large circulation women's magazines frequently carry pieces on this issue.

Prevention strategies, although hard to measure in their individual impact, lie at the heart of reducing the rates of feminicide in Brazil. It is also a very diffuse and multi-faceted activity that requires the participation of many different kinds of social institution across the country – educational, religious, commercial, political, and criminal justice – not just in propagating messages of gender equality outwards, to the general public, but also in examining their own internal practices and cultures of gender discrimination. The second is undoubtedly a harder task.

NOTES

1. In a few states in the North and North-East – Bahia, Amazonas, Sergipe, and Roraima – police patrols are referred to as *Rondas* as the word *patrulha* is associated with army patrols.

2. The partnership with the military police ended in 2015 as the latter had developed their own programme, the PPVDs. The NGO and volunteer support network continued their work with victims. http://www.sosmulherfamiliauberlandia.org.br/conheca/programa-de-abordagens-de-campo-e-domiciliares.

3. Interview, 25 May 2020.

4. Women were unable to join the military police in Brazil until the 1980s, and their entry varied by state (1986 in Rio Grande do Sul and 1990 in Bahia).

5. Interview, 25 June 2020.

6. Interview, 28 May 2020.

7. Interview with Commander of the Guard and members of the Maria da Penha patrol, December 2019.

8. The police have up to 48 hours to file the request and the court has up to 48 hours to make a decision.

9. See, for example, the Prevention of Family and Domestic Violence units (*Prevenção Orientado à Violência Doméstica e Familiar* – PROVID) set up in the Federal District, which developed directly out of community-oriented policing efforts dating back to 1991 (TJ-DFT & PMDF, 2015).

10. The 180 line was set up in 2005 by the national women's ministry (SPM) as an advice and referral line. However, in 2014 it was turned into a domestic violence hotline.

11. GPS monitoring is now in use in a number of states such as Minas Gerais and Rio de Janeiro.

12. In nearly all cases, an alert will result in the nearest patrol car (military police or municipal guard) being dispatched. Only in Acre does the *Botão da Vida* does activation result in the second response Maria da Penha patrol being sent to investigate. There, the patrol appears to respond reactively to breaches, rather than proactively with a schedule of visits.

13. For an empirical study of risk factors for female victims of homicide in Pernambuco state, see Portella (2020).

14. This process was led by Valter Shuenquener, a federal judge appointed as Advisor to the CNMP. He headed its Committee on Basic Rights, which covered work by professionals across the whole spectrum – in the courts, prosecutor's office, and public defender's office. Interview, 20 May 2020.

15. The project fell within the framework of the Sector Dialogues Support Facility entitled 'Brazil-European Union: Pathways to Fighting Domestic Violence'. https://www.sectordialogues.org/publication/at-un-event-cnmp-announces-frida-and-shares-experience-in-fight-to-stop-violence-against-women.

16. In particular, it drew on the work of the European Institute for Gender Equality (EIGE, 2019) and the experiences of Lithuania, where it is based.

17. Contained in CNJ Resolution 284 of 5 June 2019, issued at the same time as the CNMP one.

18. Personal communication by email 18 May 2020.

19. Resolução Conjunta No. 5, 3 March 2020.

20. In 2019, women constituted only 11% of active military police officers across the country. The percentage of women in the civil police was higher - 27% - due to merit-based recruitment and the absence of entry restrictions (IBGE, 2020).

21. https://agenciapatriciagalvao.org.br/violencia/violencia-domestica/pm-do-df-quer-tirar-armas-de-militares-acusados-de-violencia-domestica/.

22. Law 13.880/2019.

23. The study was carried out by Anis, a feminist research institute for bioethics, human rights, and gender.

24. Some 250,000 individuals are entitled to treatment at the hospital, which also operates clinics throughout the state for less serious cases.

25. http://www.pm.ba.gov.br/index.php?option=com_content&view=article&id=65&Itemid=66.

26. https://www.avon.com.br/instituto-avon/violencia-contra-mulheres?uam=true&mobile=4&sc=1.

Chapter Six

CONCLUSIONS

Global concern about feminicide started with the epidemic of sexualised murders and disappearances of women in Central America and Mexico. There, impunity was sustained by the apparent indifference of the authorities and a criminal justice system permeated with misogyny, institutional violence, and discrimination in the investigation process (Lagarde, 2006, p. 223; Menjívar & Walsh, 2017). However, Brazil's feminicides are overwhelmingly intimate partner homicides, and exhibit characteristics common to many countries around the world, including in the Global North. The flaws of its justice system institutions are also commonplace, and yet coalitions of interest that formed at strategic moments between women's movements, political actors, and justice-sector operators were able to break institutional inertia around feminicide. The story of the process by which these institutions were pushed to take violence against women seriously, and reform their bureaucratic and cognitive routines around feminicide and gender-based violence, can therefore yield some transferable lessons for other country contexts.

There is a saying in Brazil, 'Entre homem e mulher, não se mete a colher'. Literally translated, it says 'don't stick your spoon in' – don't interfere between husband and wife. This book demonstrates just how much that mentality has been transformed in Brazil by the combined activities of women's movements, legislators, police, prosecutors, and courts. New laws, and the innovative practices and procedures developed by the justice agencies, show that the state is now willing to 'stick its spoon' into the private sphere in situations of gender-based violence. These are positive signs that Brazil is beginning to shift from a culture of *femina sacra* – to borrow and re-gender Agamben's idea of *homo sacer* – in which women can be killed by anyone with impunity, to one of accountability and due diligence on the part of the state. This chapter lays out the key original findings of this study, drawing out the role and the interaction of the factors and processes examined throughout the book – legislation, feminist strategic action, executive branch investment, institutional capacity building, political environment, police and justice-sector leadership, and policy diffusion and influence (horizontal, vertical, and global–local).

Let's be clear – there is still a great deal of work to be done to protect women and girls from abuse. Victimisation surveys indicate that the level of sexual assault is very high in Brazil, but has not yet stimulated the kind of concerted multi-agency action witnessed since 2006 in relation to domestic violence and feminicide. It would also be impossible right now to assert that the incidence of these last two is falling, as Brazilian justice agencies are still improving their recognition processes.[1] Indeed, reports to the police of physical assault and threats in the context of domestic violence are rising, most likely due to heightened public awareness, increased confidence in the police, and better recording by the police.[2] Prevention of gender-based violence is a complex and multi-faceted task that requires concerted action across society, beyond what the criminal justice system alone can achieve.

That said, the appreciative enquiry approach adopted in this book sought to document and value the considerable advances that *have* occurred within state institutions, both national and local, in response to women's demands for protection and justice. Despite the myriad shortcomings of Brazil's criminal justice system (police brutality and racism, poor police training, low clear-up rates for many crimes, and a slow court system), the UN chose to trial the Model Protocol in Brazil in recognition of the considerable competencies in dealing with domestic violence that its criminal justice system had been embedding since 2006. This institutional capacity then enabled speedier and fuller police investigation of feminicide, acceleration of cases through the courts, inter-institutional co-operation, and law enforcement and justice-sector engagement in the local protection networks set up by women activists working inside and outside the state.

A southern criminology perspective allows us to see the ways in which criminal justice institutions of the Global South are capable of policy and practice innovations from which the Global North can learn; the flow of policy diffusion and transfer should not be assumed to be unidirectional, from North to South. In 2018, as part of the Avon Institute/FBSP project identifying innovative practices by Brazil's law enforcement agencies in combatting violence against women, I accompanied a group of the prize winners to visit the Metropolitan police in London. In this exchange of professional experiences, it transpired that practices developed and diffused in Brazil, such as the Maria da Penha patrols, were possibly more effective at deterring repeat victimisation than UK police strategies. There is also an internal colonial effect in criminological knowledge production within Brazil linked to the economic, political, and demographic dominance of major metropolitan centres such as São Paulo, Rio de Janeiro, Porto Alegre, Belo Horizonte, and Brasília, where many key research institutions (universities and independent thinktanks) are located, which reinforces epistemic exclusion. This book highlights good practice 'at the margins,' as Avon and the FBSP have done, examining how the activities of policy entrepreneurs in further-flung corners of Brazil have influenced procedures across the country.

POLICY INNOVATION AND DIFFUSION

This study shows that criminological knowledge is produced not only by academic institutions, but also by law enforcement professionals, who have together formed communities of practice. Police 'pracademics' have been key policy entrepreneurs, detecting patterns of domestic violence and feminicide within the military police, mapping repeat domestic victimisation, analysing the quantitative and qualitative impact of the Maria da Penha patrols on the security of victims, and developing new working practices for investigating feminicide through team-based, qualitative case analysis. The roots of many policy initiatives introduced to tackle gender-based violence lie in the combination of police experience in the field and their exposure to, and use of, research techniques and data analysis. In the 2000s, the PT-led federal government invested heavily in making higher education accessible to police officers, and a criterion for advancement. Through the National Network of Advanced Study in Public Security, set up in 2004, universities nationwide offered certificated post-graduate programmes. By 2010, 85 programmes in public security, human rights and citizenship were delivered by 63 higher education institutions, benefitting thousands of police officers (Lima et al., 2014). These continuing professional development programmes started to change police culture, at least in the higher ranks, and have so far survived the Bolsonaro administration, despite its hostility towards higher education establishments.[3]

Partnerships with universities have oriented police and public security specialists more towards evidence- and data-led approaches to violence reduction. This reflects the indirect influence of North American-style methodologies of quantitative data collection, analysis, and application, such as hot-spot and hot-dot analysis of victimisation. During the PT governments, the national government unit for law enforcement (*Secretaria Nacional de Segurança Pública –* SENASP) invested in encouraging multiple stakeholders across government and civil society to engage in a problem-solving approach to violence reduction.

Indeed, the states that have made the greatest strides in instigating practices tailored to tackling feminicide had all previously adopted multi-sector violence reduction strategies targeted at specific locations or victim groups.

Transforming knowledge into new policies and practice requires leadership. This has come from police pracademics and from women officers rising up the ranks. Individual officers have acted as policy influencers, responsible for the horizontal diffusion of policies such as the Maria da Penha patrols and specialist feminicide investigation units. This visible role, attracting national and international recognition, also enabled them to secure their initiatives against criticism or marginalisation within their own police force. Institutional culture is like a tanker, slow to turn around, as each new generation of recruits is socialised into the corporation's norms, attitudes, and practices. Police innovators needed support from the superiors at the top of the police hierarchy, as well as from a wider set of influential political and judicial actors. In Piauí, for example, the political backing came from the feminist vice-governor, Margarete Coelho. In many states, it was the appellate court that championed both police- and judicial-sector action on feminicide, with the middle and upper ranks of the judiciary progressively stepping up as policy promoters when the national government infrastructure for women was dismantled after 2016. Within the justice sector, diffusion of good practice has been more vertical and uniform, due to the existence of national governing bodies (CNJ and CNMP), and collegial entities for the heads of the state prosecutor's office and public defender's office. This contrasts with diffusion within the police community of practice, which has been more organic, horizontal, and uneven.

WOMEN'S MOVEMENTS AND TRANSNATIONAL ACTORS

Without a doubt the most important actor in transforming attitudes to gender-based violence has been the Brazilian women's movement in its many configurations over the decades. Several times its activism forced changes in law, jurisprudence, and criminal justice practice and proceedings. In the 1920s, women writers raised the issue of crimes of passion, which prompted male jurists to alter the 1940 criminal code. In the 1970s and 1980s, women campaigned against the so-called 'honour defence', which moved the STJ to rule this inadmissible in 1991. The creation, by male jurists, of new minor misdemeanour courts (JECrims) that could not handle domestic violence appropriately, led to a coalition of feminist jurists taking an unprecedented lead in mapping out an alternative. Their activism, and strategic engagement in legislative and policymaking spaces at all levels, also forced the justice institutions to step up. As one senior police officer commented to me, 'No police force would ever decide of its own accord to make violence against women a priority. They only do so because of pressure from women's groups'.

This pressure was amplified by transnational linkages between the Brazilian women's movement, its counterparts in the region, and supra-national governance bodies in the UN and the inter-American system. Women's NGOs have long been closely involved in hemispheric networks, and this enabled the feminist coalition to use the regional human rights system to leverage policy change at home. The IACHR's 2001 ruling on the Maria da Penha case created a critical juncture lending external impetus to the eponymous law. International presence, in the form of UN Women, was also critical to the drafting and passage of the feminicide law, and to transforming the Model Protocol into workable National Guidelines. The drafters of the law referred repeatedly to the recommendations of international bodies, to Brazil's international commitments, and to its dilatory attitude to implementation and reporting. In the event, perhaps Brazil's late adopter status in the region in terms of its domestic violence and feminicide legislation may have benefitted the women's movement by helping it build up momentum, learn from other experiences, and harness this external pressure.

LEGISLATION AND IMPLEMENTATION

Law matters. The Maria da Penha law and the naming of feminicide as a crime made women 'speakable subjects' who could claim the protection of the state inside and outside the home. But, as the UN and the inter-American monitoring bodies have noted, implementation requires much more than a new law. Brazil's 2006 comprehensive legislation on domestic violence catalysed institutional reform as it both delineated the role of each of the justice institutions and called on them to work together, with other governmental bodies and with civil society organisations. The federal government investment that ensued created 'ripeness' within criminal justice institutions, enabling them to react relatively quickly to introduction into law of the crime of feminicide in 2015.

Police forces that had hitherto not been regarded as key in responding to domestic violence built both public-facing capacity (the Maria da Penha patrols) and inward-facing capacity (training, gender units, and support for victims and abusers within their ranks). They began to engage in much-needed inter-force collaboration, sharing information on women at risk of feminicide. To ensure enforcement of protection orders, they worked more closely with the judicial branch and its new architecture (the specialist domestic violence courts), with the dedicated units set up by the justice agencies, and with the local multi-agency protection networks. Many of these advances relied on political support from women in strategic political and administrative posts. Although women's presence in elected office in Brazil is still relatively low, the *bancadas femininas* in the legislatures at all three levels of government, along with the state- and municipal-level policy bodies for women's rights (*coordenadorias*) and civil society consultation mechanism (*conselhos*), made gender-based violence a public policy priority. They were often decisive in securing enabling legislation and budget allocations, and thus to the replication of good practice.

POLITICAL ENVIRONMENT

How much is all this progress threatened by the Bolsonaro government? Political environments can be contradictory. Women in Mexico expected that the election of centre-left President Andrés Manuel López Obrador would create a policy space for the movement to work with the criminal justice system and government on that country's feminicide crisis. In the event, they were severely disappointed. Although the president brought an unprecedented number of women into his cabinets, he embarked simultaneously on a campaign of denial in relation to feminicide. His response to thousands of women taking to the streets in March 2020 was to question the statistics, dismissing them as exaggerated and 'fake'. He further alleged that the right-wing opposition had co-opted this feminist agenda as a way of bringing down his government. He continued to insist that specific interventions against feminicide, such as those adopted in Brazil, were unnecessary as more attention should be given to root causes of violence. These, he suggested, were unemployment, low wages, poor moral values, and family breakdown, reflecting his religiosity and neatly marrying left-wing and right-wing explanations of gender-based violence. By alluding to such broad, and vague, macro-level structural causes, he effectively absolved his government of taking the necessary meso-level policy measures.

Conversely, anyone following the trajectory of Bolsonaro and his government in Brazil, from his presidential election campaign based on fake news and moral panics, to his hostility to feminism and overt misogyny, might expect public policy on gender-based violence to be upended. He did immediately dismantle several parts of the human rights protection architecture in government, leaving minority groups exposed. The SPM, which had invested heavily in building capacity around violence against women, was downgraded and folded into a new ministry where protection of 'the family' (in a very restricted and conservative sense) predominated. And he continued to harp on about the dangers of 'gender ideology', using it as fresh meat for his shrinking political base. Even in the midst of the Covid-19 crisis, in May 2020, he declared it a priority to pass a government bill outlawing teaching about gender in schools. However, the word 'gender' seems to exist in two parallel universes in Brazil. When 'gender ideology' is invoked, always in relation to education, it refers almost exclusively to LGBT identities, not to gender relations between men and women. Yet, the criminal justice and governmental bodies engaging in tackling gender-based violence have no problem discussing gender roles and power relations and understand that LGBT individuals are also protected by existing legislation, even in the absence of specific new legislation.[4]

The Bolsonaro government has not undone legislation on domestic violence or feminicide despite the fact that both laws are feminist in their underlying philosophy and challenge to patriarchal social norms. The Maria da Penha law contains many non-penal provisions that are rights based, intended to restore women's right to a life free of violence, and to alter the behaviour and mentality of perpetrators (Campos, 2008). Equally the feminicide law is worded to define this violence as an act of misogyny and gender discrimination, despite the excision of the bogey word 'gender' by the religious right. So, why has the Bolsonaro government left this legislation alone? The first reason is that the penal populism of the right coincides with a strand of feminist punitivism, which supports wider and more severe criminalisation of gender-based violence. The Maria da Penha law upped penalties for domestic violence, as the 2015 anti-feminicide legislation did for some female homicides. That might explain how the latter passed in the midst of a dramatic swing to the right in parliament. However, there is a debate amongst feminist critical legal scholars about the wisdom of giving the state even more extensive penal power, particularly in a criminal justice system that is dysfunctional in so many ways, with an overloaded prison system and unaccountable police forces (Carvalho & Campos, 2011).

Conservative support for Bolsonaro is composed of at least three distinct strands: authoritarian, religious, and economic, which do not necessarily converge on all issues. Many of his electors have nostalgia for a social world that is hierarchical and patriarchal, and in which violence is permissible against 'outsider' social groups. Backing for the criminalisation, policing, and punishment of domestic violence and feminicide can be interpreted, from an authoritarian conservative perspective, as a 'tough on crime' position, protecting innocent and vulnerable women and children. The Bolsonaro government, wedded ideologically to loosening gun controls, even passed a law allowing firearms to be removed from domestic abusers because the latter can be cast as 'bad guys'. This is the point at which paternalism and feminist demands on the penal state intersect, like it or not, in policy terms. *Bolsonarismo* has a broad base of support amongst the military police, and promoting bills to set up Maria da Penha patrols and to further penalise domestic violence, sexual harassment, and sexual assault is a common activity of legislators, including former law enforcement officials, elected to political office on Bolsonaro's coat tails.[5] In a society as divided as Brazil's, various factors place individuals on the wrong side of the 'deserving and innocent line', and one is race. *Bolsonarismo* makes no secret of its white supremacist sympathies, and his appointments to institutions intended to support the rights of the black population have been controversial and openly denied the existence of structural racism. Political violence against black women has grown, encouraged on social media.[6] This makes it far harder to develop public policies to tackle the disproportionate number of black women who are victims of feminicide.

The second strand of Bolsonaro's conservative base is religious, with somewhat contradictory views on violence against women. Many of the police officers and justice officials who built new infrastructure and practices for combating domestic violence and feminicide have strong, motivating religious beliefs around protection of the vulnerable. Criminalisation of these offences leads them to support removing the offender from the family home and applying punitive sanctions and controls. However, conservative Christians also regard women as having specific obligations within the family that compete with their rights to autonomy and protection. Fundamentalist neo-Pentecostal Christians preach a biblically based patriarchy, in which men are the head of the family. Abused women frequently turn to their churches and pastors for advice, and many will hear that women should put up with violence in the name of family unity and obedience to their husbands. However, this is not a uniquely Evangelical position: a study of a Catholic organisation providing support to abused women found exactly this position propagated (Beecheno, 2019). These two competing worldviews are reflected in the confusing pronouncements of the Minister of Women, the Family, and Human Rights, which oscillated between victim blaming and supporting tougher penalties.

Although national laws on gender-based violence have been left untouched, budgets have not. The country is in a deep recession and Bolsonaro has directed resources towards his pet projects, for instance, away from education and towards the military. The budget for the women's secretariat, now within the Ministry of Women, the Family and Human Rights, plummeted from R$119 million (approximately £24 million) to R$5.3 million (£1 million). In February 2020, the president declared that funding for gender violence programming was unnecessary because what was really needed was attitudinal change.

Through the period of the Covid-19 pandemic, less than 5% of earmarked federal funds for domestic violence were released.

The first two years of the Bolsonaro government demonstrated that its rhetoric often outstripped its actions due to inexperience, unwillingness to govern, and incompetence in using policy levers in a systematic manner. It is also disconnected from the networks of policy entrepreneurs who have been building up the many anti-feminicide initiatives detailed throughout this book. This disconnection has led the Ministry of Women, the Family and Human Rights to reinvent well-functioning wheels: it organised a conference for leaders of the Maria da Penha police patrols just weeks after the key multiplier of this programme held a similar event in Bahia; in June 2020, the Ministry launched a new protocol for investigating feminicide despite the fact that the National Guidelines have existed since 2016; and in December 2020, the President signed a decree creating a multi-agency working group on feminicide much like the one had worked so successfully in 2016.

Whilst a lot of damage was done to Brazil's institutions by politicised federal executive appointments and interventions, the country's federalised structure of government, with public policy largely enacted at state and municipal levels, provided something of a buffer in the short term. The money and energy invested in local government violence reduction programmes between 2003 and 2014 embedded ways of thinking and working that have been resilient to the scattergun rhetorical barrage of *bolsonarismo*, especially in areas of the country governed by more centrist or centre-left administrations. In addition, the historical autonomy of the judicial agencies gives them more immunity than the police to political interference and ideological re-orientation.

Due to decades of women's movement campaigning and engagement with state institutions, combating violence against women and feminicide now has very broad political-, social-, and justice-sector support. This was noticeable during the Covid-19 crisis of 2020–2021 when police and justice institutions acted quickly to try and mitigate the inevitable rise in domestic violence and feminicides that accompanied orders for people to stay at home. Civil police precincts switched to allowing online registration of crimes, the domestic violence patrols made daily phone calls to women holding restraining orders, and the CNJ, Brazilian Magistrates Association and police forces around the country supported a 'red alert' campaign, orienting women to silently report abuse in pharmacies where they could be referred for assistance. It is to be hoped that this embedded capacity with the criminal justice agencies and their civil society partners in local protection networks will endure through the pressures of the pandemic, economic recession and, possibly, political upheaval.

CHALLENGES

There is still a long way to go to adequately address gender-based violence and feminicide. Whilst work on feminicide prevention and investigation will continue in the state and municipal governments, funded largely from local budgets, they face ongoing challenges of improving co-ordination both horizontally, between different agencies and branches of government, and vertically, between the levels of government. Offering more universal and uniform protection to victims of gender-based violence across the country is problematic in a federalised country that now lacks strong central institutions advocating for women's rights and for a human rights-based approach to public safety. The need to join up the current patchwork of institutions into an effective network is still hindered by a degree of competition, incoherence, and lack of information sharing amongst the criminal justice agencies. The pioneering approaches undertaken by individual policy innovators need to be furthered mainstreamed and institutionalised.

In terms of legislation, there remains a serious loophole in the criminal code – the unfair provocation and violent emotion clause – that allows men who murder women to get off scot-free. Removing this will require a whole new round of strategic feminist engagement with political, legal, and judicial actors. This raises the question of how influential feminist ideas and actors are within judicial and law enforcement institutions, and what can be achieved within them. More women than ever are entering the police and moving into the upper echelons of the judiciary. This, in itself, is no guarantee of a particular stance because women need to be critical actors as well as a critical mass. However, they often prove to be key allies to civil society demands mobilised outside these institutions.

Debates within the critical feminist criminological community, especially about the traps of pursuing 'carceral feminism' (Goodmark, 2018), indicate the dangers of believing that justice institutions can change social relations, as they are only one small part of the wider cultural transformation that is needed. Whilst it is laudable that police officers and justice officials have set up programmes to visit schools, awareness raising and prevention of gender-based violence need to be mainstreamed into the curriculum at all levels. This is challenging whilst *bolsonarista* conservatives insist on turning education and social debate around gender relations and around human rights into a political battleground. This hostile political environment also affects the protection of vulnerable and minority women, such as black, indigenous, rural, and transgender women, as well as women caught up in the violence connected to criminal actors in poor neighbourhoods. As Stoever (2019) notes, when safety is politicised, not all women will receive equal protection.

Each of the elements analysed here – women's movement, law, political environment, and criminal justice institutions – has been determinant, but not sufficient on its own, in the process of shaping state responses in Brazil to feminicide and gender-based violence, as they interact in complex and iterative ways. But perhaps the clearest lesson of this story for other countries in Latin America, and beyond, is that when women claim space and act strategically in public discourse, in lawmaking, in criminal justice institutions, in politics, and in policymaking, they can transform the actions and attitudes of government and society towards the violence that blights and ends the lives of so many women and girls.

NOTES

1. In 2019, the police recorded 66,123 reported rapes (of which 85.7% involved female victims) (FBSP, 2020a, p. 128).

2. In 2019, police logged 266,310 domestic violence-related assaults, up 5% on 2018, whilst threats rose 9%, to 498,597 (FBSP, 2020a, pp. 124, 126).

3. See, for example, Silva (2020), an edited volume of Master's-level dissertation research on the Maria da Penha law, feminicide, and policing conducted by military police officers in the Federal District and Goiás state.

4. Although trans women and lesbians are protected by the Maria da Penha and feminicide laws, PLS 122/2006, which would have criminalised homophobia, got stuck in the Senate for eight years and was finally shelved in 2014. The Supreme Court ruled in June 2019 that anti-LGBT hate crime should be dealt with as analogous to the hate crime of racism. The neo-Pentecostal caucus in Congress drafted their own bill to define the murder of LGBT people as aggravated homicide, just like feminicide, but still allow the kinds of discriminatory speech that can lead to such hate crimes.

5. My observation from surveying the significant number of law enforcement officials entering politics in the last decade, and the kinds of legislative activities they engage in. Many also promote bills on animal rights and disability rights, consistent with their self-image as protectors of those who are regarded as vulnerable and, crucially, unthreatening.

6. A study showed that 81% of victims of online racism were middle class, educated black women aged 20–35 (Trindade, 2018).

REFERENCES

Abramovich, V. (2011). Responsabilidad estatal por violencia de género: Comentarios sobre el caso 'Campo Algodonero' en la Corte Interamericana de Derechos Humanos. *Anuario de Derechos Humanos*, 6, 167–182. doi:10.5354/0718-2279.2011

ACADEPOL. (2019). *Feminicídios: Diretrizes para o atendimento de local de crime e investigação de mortes violentas de mulheres.* São Paulo: Academia de Polícia.

ACUNS. (2017). *Femicide VII: Establishing a femicide watch in every country.* Vienna: Academic Council on the United Nations System, Vienna Liaison Office.

Alvarez, S. E. (1990). *Engendering democracy in Brazil: Women's movements in transition politics.* Princeton, NJ: Princeton University Press.

Amnesty International. (2003). *Intolerable killings: 10 years of abductions and murders of women in Ciudad Juárez and Chihuahua.* London: Amnesty International: AMR 41/026/2003.

Angotti, B., & Vieira, R. S. C. (2020). O processo de tipificação do feminicídio no Brasil. In P. T. M. Bertolin, B. Angotti, & R. S. C. Vieira (Eds.), *Feminicídio: quando a desigualdade de gênero mata: Mapeamento da tipificação na América Latina* (pp. 35–70). Joaçaba: Editora Unoesc.

Auras, A. T. (2020). A implementação de políticas públicas de enfrentamento à violência doméstica e familiar contra a mulher em Santa Catarina: Desafios e perspectivas. In J. M. Xaud, L. P. Landim, & R. B. R. Oliveira (Eds.), *Defensoria pública: reflexões sobre os direitos das mulheres* (pp. 13–26). Brasília: ANADEP.

Ávila, T. P. (2018). The criminalisation of femicide. In S. Walklate, K. Fitz-Gibbon, J. McCulloch, & J. Maher (Eds.), *Intimate partner violence, risk and security: Securing women's lives in a global world* (pp. 181–198). New York, NY: Routledge.

Bandeira, L. (2009). Três décadas de resistência feminista contra o sexismo e a violência feminina no Brasil: 1976 a 2006. *Sociedade e Estado*, 24(2), 401–438. doi:10.1590/S0102-69922009000200004

Bandeira, L. M., & Almeida, T. M. C. (2015). Vinte anos da Convenção de Belém do Pará e a Lei Maria da Penha. *Revista de Estudos Feministas*, 23(2), 501–517. doi:10.1590/0104-026X2015v23n2p501

Barsted, L. L. (2011). Lei Maria da Penha: Uma experiência bem-sucedida de advocacy feminista. In C. H. Campos (Ed.), *Lei Maria da Penha comentada em uma perspectiva jurídico-feminista* (pp. 13–37). Rio de Janeiro: Editora Lumen Juris.

Beecheno, K. (2019). Faith-based organisations as welfare providers in Brazil: The conflict over gender in cases of domestic violence. *Social Inclusion*, 7(2), 14–23. doi:10.17645/si.v7i2

Beiras, A., Nascimento, M., & Incrocci, C. (2019). Programs for men who have used violence against women: An overview of interventions in Brazil. *Saúde e Sociedade*, 28(1), 262–274. doi:10.1590/s0104-12902019170995

Benevides, B. G., & Naider Bonfim Nogueira, S. N. B. (Eds.). (2020). *Dossiê dos assassinatos e da violência contra travestis e transexuais brasileiras em 2019*. São Paulo: Expressão Popular, ANTRA, IBTE.

Bernardes, M. N., & Albuquerque, M. I. B. (2016). Violências interseccionais silenciadas em medidas protetivas de urgência. *Direito & Praxis*, 7(15), 715–740.

Besse, S. K. (1989). Crimes of passion: The campaign against wife killing in Brazil, 1910–1940. *Journal of Social History*, 22(4), 653–666. doi:10.1353/jsh/22.4.653

Bianchini, A. (2016). A qualificadora do feminicídio é de natureza objetiva ou subjetiva? *Revista da EMERJ*, 19(72), 203–219.

Borelli, A. (2005). Da privação dos sentidos à legitima defesa da honra: Considerações sobre o direito e a violência contra as mulheres. *Revista Brasileira de Ciências Criminais*, 13(54), 9–42.

Brazil. (2016). *Diretrizes nacionais para investigar, processar e julgar com perspectiva de gênero as mortes violentas de mulheres (feminicídios)*. Brasília: Secretaria de Políticas para Mulheres.

Brigagão, J. I. M. (2018). Comissão de Violência Doméstica do Hospital Militar: Belo Horizonte (MG). In FBSP (Ed.), *Práticas inovadoras de enfrentamento à violência contra as mulheres: experiências desenvolvidas pelos profissionais de segurança pública – Casoteca FBSP 2017* (pp. 89–103). São Paulo: Fórum Brasileiro de Segurança Pública.

Bueno, S., & Brigagão, J. (2018). Ronda para homens da Ronda Maria da Penha PMBA: Salvador (BA). In FBSP (Ed.), *Práticas inovadoras de enfrentamento à violência contra as mulheres: experiências desenvolvidas pelos profissionais de segurança pública – Casoteca FBSP 2017* (pp. 43–54). São Paulo: Fórum Brasileiro de Segurança Pública.

Bueno, S. & Pacheco, D. (2020). Patrulha Maria da Penha para a Tropa. In FBSP (Ed.) *Práticas de enfrentamento à violência contra as mulheres: experiências desenvolvidas pelos profissionais de segurança pública e do sistema de justiça – Casoteca FBSP 2019* (pp. 107–115). São Paulo: Fórum Brasileiro de Segurança Pública.

Bunch, C., & Frost, S. (2000). Human rights. In C. Kramarae & D. Spender (Eds.), *Routledge encyclopedia of women: Global women's issues and knowledge* (pp. 1078–1083). New York, NY: Routledge.

Câmara dos Deputados. (1993). *Comissão Parlamentar de Inquérito destinada a investigar a questão da violência contra a mulher: Relatório Final*. Brasília: Federal Chamber of Deputies.

Campos, C. H. (2003). Juizados Especiais Criminais e seu déficit teórico. *Revista de Estudos Feministas, 11*(1), 155–170.

Campos, C. H. (2008). Lei Maria da Penha: Mínima intervenção punitiva, máxima intervenção social. *Revista Brasileira de Ciências Criminais, 73*, 244–267.

Campos C. H. (Ed.). (2011). *Lei Maria da Penha comentada em uma perspectiva jurídico-feminista*. Rio de Janeiro: Editora Lumen Juris.

Campos, C. H. (2015). A CPMI da violência contra a mulher e a implementação da Lei Maria da Penha. *Revista Estudos Feministas, 23*(2), 519–531. doi:10.1590/0104-026X2015v23n2p519

Campos, C. H., & Carvalho, S. (2006). Violência doméstica e Juizados Especiais Criminais: Análise a partir do feminismo e do garantismo. *Revista Estudos Feministas, 14*(2), 409–422. doi:10.1590/S0104-026X2006000200005

Campos, C. H., & Carvalho, S. (2011). Tensões atuais entre a criminologia feminista e a crimi-nologia crítica: A experiência brasileira. In C. H. Campos (Ed.), *Lei Maria da Penha comentada em uma perspectiva jurídico-feminista* (pp. 143–169). Rio de Janeiro: Lumen Juris.

Carcedo, A., & Sagot, M. (2000). *Femicídio en Costa Rica, 1990–1999*. San José: Pan American Health Organization.

Carcedo, A. (Ed.). (2010). *No olvidamos ni aceptamos: femicidio en Centroamérica 2000–2006*. San José: Asociación Centro Feminista de Información y Acción.

Cardoso, R. B. N. (2016). *Homens autores de violência contra parceiros íntimos: Estudo com policiais militares do Distrito Federal.* Unpublished Master's dissertation in Social Development, Society and International Co-operation, University of Brasília.

Carneiro, S. (2019). Mulheres negras e violência doméstica: decodificando os números. In W. Pasinato, B. A. Machado, & T. P. Ávila (Eds.), *Políticas públicas de prevenção à violência contra a mulher* (pp. 205–224). São Paulo: Marcial Pons.

Carone, R. R. (2018). A atuação do movimento feminista no legislativo federal: Caso da Lei Maria da Penha. *Lua Nova, 105*, 181–216. doi:10.1590/0102-181216/105

Carrington, K., Guala, N., Puyol, M. V., & Sozzo, M. (2020). How women's police stations empower women, widen access to justice and prevent gender violence. *International Journal for Crime, Justice and Social Democracy, 9*(1), 42–67. doi.org/10.5204/ijcjsd.v9i1.1494

Carrington, K., Hogg, R., & Sozzo, M. (2016). Southern criminology. *British Journal of Criminology, 56*(1), 1–20. doi:10.1093/bjc/azv083

CEDAW. (1992). General recommendation No. 19: Violence against women. UN Committee on the Elimination of Discrimination Against Women. Retrieved from https://www.ohchr.org/en/hrbodies/cedaw/pages/recommendations.aspx

CEDAW. (2003). Report of the UN Committee on the Elimination of Discrimination against Women, Twenty-eighth session (13–31 January 2003), Twenty-ninth session (30 June–18 July 2003), 18 August 2003, A/58/38. Retrieved from https://www.refworld.org/docid/4176705e4.html

Celorio, R. M. (2010). González ('Cotton Field') v. Mexico (Inter-Am. Ct. H.R.), Introductory note. *International Legal Materials, 49*(3), 637–761.

CNJ. (2019a). *Relatório estatístico: Mês Nacional do Júri 2018.* Brasília: Conselho Nacional de Justiça.

CNJ. (2019b). *Justiça em números.* Brasília: Conselho Nacional de Justiça.

CNJ. (2020). *Relatório: Mês Nacional do Júri 2019.* Brasília: Conselho Nacional de Justiça.

CNMP. (2019). *Manual de atuação das promotoras e dos promotores de justiça em casos de feminicídio.* Brasília: Conselho Nacional do Ministério Público.

Corrêa, M. (1981). *Os crimes da paixão*. São Paulo: Brasiliense.

Corrêa, M. (1983). *Morte em família: Representações jurídicas de papéis sexuais*. Rio de Janeiro: Graal.

Deus, A., & Gonzalez, D. (2018). *Analysis of femicide/feminicide legislation in Latin America and the Caribbean and a proposal for a model law*. Panama: MESECVI/UN Women.

Diniz, D., Costa, B., & Gumieri, S. (2015). Nomear feminicídio: conhecer, simbolizar e punir. *Revista Brasileira de Ciências Criminais, 114*, 225–239.

Diniz, D., & Gumieri, S. (2016). Implementação de medidas protetivas da Lei Maria da Penha no Distrito Federal entre 2006 e 2012. In A. C. C. Pareschi, C. L. Engel, & G. C. Baptista (Eds.), *Direitos humanos, grupos vulneráveis e segurança pública* (pp. 205–231). Brasília: Ministério da Justiça e Cidadania, Secretaria Nacional de Segurança Pública (Coleção Pensando a Segurança Pública vol. 6).

ECOSOC. (1997). Report of the Special Rapporteur on Violence Against Women: Mission to Brazil, E/CN.4/1997/47/Add.2. United Nations Economic and Social Council. Retrieved from https://www.ohchr.org/en/issues/women/srwomen/pages/annualreports.aspx

ECOSOC. (2013). Vienna declaration on femicide statement submitted by the Academic Council on the United Nations System (ACUNS), E/CN.15/2013/NGO/1. Retrieved from https://www.ohchr.org/en/issues/women/srwomen/pages/annualreports.aspx.

EIGE. (2019). *A guide to risk assessment and risk management of intimate partner violence against women for police*. Vilnius: European Institute for Gender Equality.

Engel, M. G. (2000). Paixão, crime e relações de gênero (Rio de Janeiro, 1890–1930). *Topoi, 1*(1), 153–177. doi:10.1590/2237-101X001001004

Eluf, L. N. (2007). *A paixão no banco dos réus: Casos passionais célebres* (3rd ed.). São Paulo: Saraiva.

FBSP. (2015). *As mulheres nas instituições policiais*. São Paulo: Fórum Brasileiro de Segurança Pública.

FBSP. (2019). *Anuário Brasileiro de Segurança Pública 13*. São Paulo: Fórum Brasileiro de Segurança Pública.

FBSP. (2020a). *Anuário Brasileiro de Segurança Pública 14*. São Paulo: Fórum Brasileiro de Segurança Pública.

FBSP. (2020b). *Princípios e práticas de formação de policiais para o atendimento às mulheres em situação de violência*. São Paulo: Fórum Brasileiro de Segurança Pública.

FBSP/Pulse. (2020). *Politíca e fé entre os policiais militares, civis, e federais do Brasil*. São Paulo: Fórum Brasileiro de Segurança Pública.

Frazer, E., & Hutchings, E. (2019). The feminist politics of naming violence. *Feminist Theory, 1*(2), 199–216. doi:10.1177/1464700119859759

Freeman, M. A., Chinkin, C., & Rudolf, B. (Eds.). (2012). *The UN Convention on the Elimination of all Forms of Discrimination Against Women: A commentary*. Oxford: Oxford University Press.

Fregoso, R.-L., & Bejarano, C. (Eds.). (2010). *Terrorizing women: Feminicide in the Americas*. Durham, NC: Duke University Press.

Friedman, E. J. (2009). Re(gion)alizing women's human rights in Latin America. *Politics & Gender, 5*(3), 349–375. doi:10.1017/S1743923X09990171

Gerhard, N. (2014). *Patrulha Maria da Penha: O impacto da ação da Polícia Militar no enfrentamento da violência doméstica*. Porto Alegre: AGE/EDIPUCRS.

Goodmark, L. (2018). *Decriminalizing domestic violence: A balanced policy approach to intimate partner violence*. Berkeley, CA: University of California Press.

Grossi, P. K., & Spaniol, M. I. (2019). Patrulhas Maria da Penha no Estado do Rio Grande do Sul: análise dos avanços e desafios dos cinco anos da experiência pioneira desta política pública de prevenção à violência de gênero. In W. Pasinato, B. A. Machado, & T. P. Ávila (Eds.), *Políticas públicas de prevenção à violência contra a mulher* (pp. 298–328). São Paulo: Marcial Pons.

Hautzinger, S. J. (2007). *Violence in the city of women: Police and batterers in Bahia, Brazil*. Berkeley, CA: University of California Press.

Heinrich Böll Stiftung. (2017). *Feminicide: A global phenomenon from Brussels to San Salvador*. Brussels: Heinrich Böll Stiftung.

Hill, J. (2019). *See what you made me do: Power, control and domestic abuse*. Carlton: Black Inc.

Human Rights Watch. (1991). *Criminal injustice: Violence against women in Brazil*. New York, NY: Americas Watch/Human Rights Watch.

IACHR. (2001). Maria da Penha Maia Fernandes v. Brazil, Case 12.051, Report No. 54/01, OEA/Ser.L./III.111, doc. 20 1-2 (2000), issued 16 April 2001. Inter-American Commission on Human Rights.

IBGE. (2020). *Pesquisa de Informações Básicas Estaduais – ESTADIC, 2019*. Brasília: Instituto Brasileira de Estatística e Geografia.

Instituto Patrícia Galvão. (2006). *Percepção e reações da sociedade sobre a violência contra a mulher*. São Paulo: Instituto Patrícia Galvão.

Instituto Patrícia Galvão. (2013). *Percepção da sociedade sobre violência e assassinatos de mulheres* Sao Paulo: Instituto Patrícia Galvão.

IPEA/FBSP. (2020). *Atlas da violência*. Rio de Janeiro: Instituto de Pesquisa Econômica Aplicada and São Paulo: Fórum Brasileiro de Segurança Pública.

Kaufman, M. (2001). The White Ribbon campaign: Involving men and boys in ending global violence against women. In B. Pease & K. Pringle (Eds.), *A man's world? Changing men's practices in a globalized world* (pp. 38–51). New York, NY: Zed Books.

Keck, M. E., & Sikkink, K. (1998). *Activists beyond borders: Advocacy networks in international politics*. Ithaca, NY: Cornell University Press.

Lacey, N. (1998). *Unspeakable subjects: Feminist essays in legal and social theory*. Oxford: Hart Publishing.

Lagarde, M. (2006). Del femicidio al feminicidio. *Desde el Jardin de Freud, 6*, 216–225.

Lavigne, R. M. R. (2011). Caso Fonaje: o ativismo de juízes integrantes do Fórum Nacional dos Juizados Especiais no processo de elaboração da Lei Maria da Penha. In C. H. Campos (Ed.), *Lei Maria da Penha comentada em uma perspectiva jurídico-feminista* (pp. 65–92). Rio de Janeiro: Editora Lumen Juris.

Leão, I. V. (2019). Igualdade de gênero no curriculo escolar: Os significados na Lei Maria da Penha até a judicialização da política educacional. In W. Pasinato, B. A. Machado, & T. P. Ávila (Eds.), *Políticas públicas de prevenção à violência contra a mulher* (pp. 47–71). São Paulo: Marcial Pons.

Lima, R. K. (2010). Sensibilidades jurídicas, saber e poder: Bases culturais de alguns aspectos do direito brasileiro em uma perspectiva comparada. *Anuário Antropológico, II*, 25–51. doi:10.4000/aa.885

Lima, R. S., Carbonari, F., Figueiredo, L., & Pröglhöf, P. (2014). Avaliação de resultados da Rede Nacional de Altos Estudos em Segurança Pública – Renaesp. In C. S. L. Lima et al. (Eds.), *Avaliações, diagnósticos e análises de ações, programas e projetos em segurança pública* (pp. 187–223). Brasília: Ministério da Justiça, Secretaria Nacional de Segurança Pública.

Lyra, R. (1935). *O suicídio frustro e a responsabilidade dos criminosos passionais*. Rio de Janeiro: SCP.

Macaulay, F. (2000a). Tackling violence against women in Brazil: Converting international principles into effective local policy. In S. Jacobs, R. Jacobson, & J. Marchbank (Eds.), *States of conflict: Gender, violence and resistance* (pp. 144–62). London: Zed Press.

Macaulay, F. (2000b). Getting gender on the policy agenda: A study of a Brazilian feminist lobby group. In E. Dore & M. Molyneux (Eds.), *The hidden histories of gender and the state in Latin America* (pp. 346–367). Durham, NC: Duke University Press.

Macaulay, F. (2005). Private conflicts, public powers: Domestic violence inside and outside the courts in Latin America. In A. Angell, L. Schjolden, & R. Sieder (Eds.), *The judicialization of politics in Latin America* (pp. 211–230). London: Palgrave/Institute for the Study of the Americas.

Macaulay, F. (2006). *Gender politics in Brazil and Chile: The role of political parties in local and national policy-making.* London: Palgrave/St Antony's.

Macaulay, F. (2010). Trickling up, down and sideways: Gender policy and political opportunity in Brazil. In N. Lebon & E. Maier (Eds.), *Women's activism in Latin America and the Caribbean: Engendering social justice, democratizing citizenship* (pp. 273–288). New Brunswick, NJ: Rutgers University Press.

Macaulay, F. (2017). Dilma Rousseff (2011-16): A crisis of governance and consensus in Brazil. In V. Montecinos (Ed.). *Women presidents and prime ministers in post-transition democracies* (pp. 123–140). New York, NY: Palgrave.

Machado, M. D. C. (2018). O discurso cristão sobre a 'ideologia de gênero'. *Revista Estudos Feministas, 26*(2). doi:10.1590/1806-9584-2018v26n247463

Machado, M. R. A. (Ed.). (2015). *A violência doméstica fatal: O problema do feminicídio íntimo no Brasil.* Brasília: Ministério da Justiça/Cejus/FGV.

Maciel, D. A. (2011). Ação coletiva, mobilização do direito e instituições políticas: O caso da campanha da Lei Maria da Penha. *Revista Brasileira de Ciências Sociais, 26*(77), 97–111. doi:10.1590/S0102-69092011000300010&and

Martins, J., & Machado, P. (2020). Intervenção policial em ocorrências de violência doméstica. In FBSP (Ed.) *Práticas de enfrentamento à violência contra as mulheres: experiências desenvolvidas pelos profissionais de segurança pública e do sistema de justiça – Casoteca FBSP 2019* (pp. 23–36). São Paulo: Fórum Brasileiro de Segurança Pública.

Meneghel, S. N., Bairros, F., Mueller, B., Monteiro, D., Oliveira, L. P., & Collaziol, M. E. (2011). Rotas críticas de mulheres em situação de violência:

Depoimentos de mulheres e operadores em Porto Alegre. *Cadernos de Saúde Pública*, 27(4), 743–752. doi:10.1590/S0102-311X2011000400013

Menjívar, C., & Walsh, S. D. (2017). The architecture of feminicide: The state, inequalities, and everyday gender violence in Honduras. *Latin American Research Review*. 52(2), 221–240. https://doi.org/10.25222/larr.73

MESECVI. (2008). Declaration on femicide. In *Fourth meeting of the Committee of Experts of the Mechanism to Follow Up the Convention of Belém do Pará*, OEA/Ser.L/II.7.10 MESECVI/CEVI/DEC.1/08 and CIM02232E01, August 15, 2008, Washington, DC.

MESECVI. (2012). *Second hemispheric report on the implementation of the Belém do Pará Convention*, OEA/Ser.L/II.6.10. Inter-American Commission of Women, Washington, DC.

MESECVI. (2014). *Guide to the application of the Inter-American convention on the prevention, punishment and eradication of violence against women (Belém do Pará Convention)*, OEA/Ser.L. OEA/Ser.L/II.6.14. Inter-American Commission of Women, Washington, DC.

Meyer, M. K. (1999). Negotiating international norms: The Inter-American Commission of Women and the Convention on Violence Against Women. In M. K. Meyer & E. Prügl (Eds.), *Gender politics in global governance* (pp. 58–72). Lanham, MD: Rowland and Littlefield.

Monárrez, J. (2009). *Trama de una injusticia: Feminicidio sexual sistémico en Ciudad Juárez*. Tijuana: El Colegio de la Frontera Norte and Miguel Ángel Porrúa.

Monckton Smith, J. (2019). Intimate partner femicide: Using Foucauldian analysis to track an eight stage progression to homicide. *Violence Against Women*, 26(11), 1267–1285. doi:10.1177/1077801219863876

Monckton Smith, J., Williams, A., & Mullane, F. (2014). *Domestic abuse, homicide and gender: Strategies for policy and practice*. Hampshire: Palgrave Macmillan.

Moreira, C. N. (2006). *A passar de largo: vitimização repetida e violência conjugal*. Unpublished dissertation, Specialisation course in Public Security Policies and Management, Military Police Academy and Fundação João Pinheiro, Minas Gerais.

Nelson, S. (1996). Constructing and negotiating gender in women's police stations in Brazil. *Latin American Perspectives*, 23(1), 131–148. doi: 10.1177/0094582X9602300109

Neme, C., & Martins, C. (2018). Núcleo de Estudo e Pesquisa em Violência de Gênero e Núcleo Policial Investigativo de Feminícidio: Teresina (PI). In *FBSP Práticas inovadoras de enfrentamento à violência contra as mulheres: Experiências desenvolvidas pelos profissionais de segurança pública – Casoteca FBSP 2017*. São Paulo: Fórum Brasileiro de Segurança Pública.

Oliveira, C. F. S. (2017). *Do pensamento feminista ao código penal: O processo de criação da Lei do Feminicídio no Brasil*. Unpublished Master's dissertation, Faculty of Philosophy and Human Sciences, Federal University of Bahia, Salvador.

OPESP. (2019). *Análise crítica sobre suicídio policial*. São Paulo: Ouvidoria da Polícia do Estado de São Paulo.

Paiva, L. F. S. (2019). 'Aqui não tem gangue, tem facção': As transformações sociais do crime em Fortaleza, Brasil. *Caderno CRH, 32*(85), 165–184.

Paredes, M. (2017). Major Denice Santiago: Uma mulher negra e feminista num lugar de poder da Polícia Militar da Bahia. *Cadernos de Gênero e Diversidade, 3*(2), 48–69. doi:10.9771/cgd.v3i2.22781

Pasinato, W. (2011). 'Feminicídios' e as mortes de mulheres no Brasil. *Cadernos Pagu, 37*, 217–246. doi:10.1590/S0104-83332011000200008

Pasinato, W., Machado, B. A., & Ávila, T. P. (Eds.). (2019). *Políticas públicas de prevenção à violência contra a mulher*. São Paulo: Marcial Pons.

Penha, M. (1994). *Sobrevivi… posso contar*. Fortaleza: Conselho Cearense dos Direitos da Mulher.

Pereira, E. G., & Ferreira, G. A. (2017). A violência doméstica contra a mulher sob a ótica da vitimização repetida: Uma análise da atuação do serviço de prevenção à violência doméstica. *O Alferes, 71*(27), 133–169.

Pimentel, S., Pandjiarjian, V., & Belloque, J. (2006). Legítima defesa da honra. Ilegítima impunidade de assassinos: Um estudo crítico da legislação e jurisprudência na América Latina. In M. Corrêa & E. R. Souza (Eds.), *Vida em família: Uma perspectiva comparativa sobre 'crimes de honra'* (pp. 65–134). Campinas: Núcleo de Estudos de Gênero-Pagu/Unicamp.

Pires, A. A. (2015). A natureza objetiva da qualificadora do feminicídio e sua quesitação no Tribunal do Júri. Portal JusBrasil. Retrieved from https://amomalbernaz.jusbrasil.com.br/artigos/172762972/a-natureza-objetiva-da-qualificadora-do-feminicidio-e-sua-quesitacao-no-tribunal-do-juri. Accessed on March 10, 2015.

Pitanguy, J. (2018). Carta das Mulheres Brasileiras aos Constituintes: Memórias para o futuro. In P. T. M. Bertolin, D. A. Andrade, & M. S. Machado (Eds.), *Carta das Mulheres Brasileiras aos Constituintes: 30 anos depois* (pp. 9–44). São Paulo: Editora Autonomia Literária.

Pivetta, L. B. D. (2020). The (il)legal limitation of women's recruitment into Brazilian military police forces. *Policing and Society.* doi:10.1080/10439463.2020.1786090

Poole, L. (2013). *Génesis de la Convención de Belém do Pará: Educar y promover el rechazo a la violencia. Suplemento Todas (Suplemento Especial octubre de 2013).* Mexico: Instituto Nacional de Mujeres de México (Inmujeres). Retrieved from http://www.oas.org/es/CIM/docs/Poole_Todas.pdf. Accessed on March 14, 2020.

Portella, A. P. (2020). *Como morre uma mulher.* Recife: Editora Universidade Federal de Pernambuco.

Radford, J., & Russell, D. E. H. (1992). *Femicide: The politics of woman killing.* Buckingham: Open University Press.

Roche, S. E., Biron, K., & Reilly, N. (1995). Sixteen days of activism against gender violence. *Violence Against Women, 1*(3), 272–281. doi:10.1177/1077801295001003007

Rodríguez, T., Montané, D., & Pulitzer, L. (2008). *Daughters of Juárez: A true story of serial murder south of the border.* New York, NY: Atria Books.

Roggeband, C. (2016). Ending violence against women in Latin America: Feminist norm setting in a multilevel context. *Politics & Gender, 12*(1), 143–167. doi:10.1017/S1743923X15000604

Rubio-Marín, R., & Sandoval, C. (2011). Engendering the reparations jurisprudence of the Inter-American Court of Human Rights: The promise of the 'Cotton Field' judgment. *Human Rights Quarterly, 33*(4), 1062–1091. doi:10.1353/hrq.2011.0060

Santos, C. M. (2005). *Women's police stations: Gender, violence and justice in São Paulo, Brazil.* New York, NY: Palgrave Macmillan.

Scarance, V. (2017). *Raio X do feminicídio em São Paulo.* São Paulo: Ministerio Público do Estado de São Paulo.

Schlittler, M. C. (2019). Programa de Instrução Maria da Penha: Grupo Reflexivo Terapêutico para Homens. In FBSP (Ed.), *Práticas de enfrentamento à violência contra as mulheres: experiências desenvolvidas pelos profissionais de segurança pública e do sistema de justiça – Casoteca FBSP 2018* (pp. 119–129). São Paulo: Fórum Brasileiro de Segurança Pública.

Schlittler, M. C., & Hanashiro, O. (2019). Projeto integrar. In FBSP (Ed.), *Práticas de enfrentamento a violência contra as mulheres: experiências desenvolvidas pelos profissionais de segurança pública e do sistema de justiça – Casoteca FBSP 2018* (pp. 93–101). São Paulo: Fórum Brasileiro de Segurança Pública.

Schritzmeyer, A. L. P. (2013). *Jogo, ritual e teatro: Um estudo antropológico do tribunal do júri*. São Paulo: Terceiro Nome.

Segato, R. (2010). Territory, sovereignty and crimes of the second state: The writing on the body of murdered women. In R.-L. Fregoso & C. Bejarano (Eds.), *Terrorizing women: Feminicide in the Americas* (pp. 70–92). Durham, NC: Duke University Press.

Senado Federal. (2013). *Comissão Parlamentar Mista de Inquérito da Violência contra a Mulher: Relatório Final*. Brasília: Federal Senate.

SENASP. (2013). *Mulheres nas instituições de segurança pública*. Brasília: Ministério da Justiça/Secretaria Nacional de Segurança Pública.

Sherman, L., Strang, H., & O'Connor, D. (2017). Introduction: Key facts about domestic abuse: Lessons from eight studies. *Cambridge Journal of Evidence-based Policing, 1*(2–3), 59–63. doi:10.1007/s41887-017-0014-y

Silva, L. L. (Ed.). (2020). *Feminicídio, violência doméstica e familiar contra a mulher sob a perspectiva policial*. Brasília: Editora Ultima Ratio.

Silvestre, G. (2020). Programa de pesquisa e capacitação continuada dos policiais civis do Estado de São Paulo em feminicídio e a investigação sob a perspectiva de gênero. In FBSP (Ed.) *Práticas de enfrentamento à violência contra as mulheres: experiências desenvolvidas pelos profissionais de segurança pública e do sistema de justiça – Casoteca FBSP 2019* (pp. 61–69). São Paulo: Fórum Brasileiro de Segurança Pública.

Šimonović, D. (2014). Global and regional standards on violence against women: The evolution and synergy of the CEDAW and Istanbul Conventions. *Human Rights Quarterly, 36*(3), 590–606.

Stoever, J. K. (2019). *The politicization of safety: Critical perspectives on domestic violence responses*. New York, NY: University Press.

Tavares, L. A., & Campos, C. H. (2018). Botão do pânico e a Lei Maria da Penha. *Revista Brasileira de Políticas Públicas, 8*(1), 397–420. doi:10.5102/rbpp.v8i1.5056

Tiroch, K. (2010). Violence against women by private actors: The Inter-American Court's judgment in the case of González et al. ('Cotton Field') v. Mexico. *Max Planck Yearbook of United Nations Law, 14*(1), 371–408. doi:10.1163/18757413-90000056

TJ-DFT & PMDF. (2015). *Relatório annual 2015*. Brasília: Tribunal de Justiça do Distrito Federal e Territórios and Polícia Militar do Distrito Federal.

Toledo, P. (2017). Criminalisation of femicide/feminicide in Latin American countries. *Rivista di Criminologia, Vittimologia e Sicurezza, 11*(2), 43–60. doi:10.14664/rcvs/724

Trindade, L. V. P. (2018). *Contemporary forms of racism and bigotry on social media platforms*. Policy Brief, University of Southampton.

UN. (1986). Report of the world conference to review and appraise the achievements of the UN decade for women: Equality, development and peace, A/CONF.116/28/Rev.1. United Nations, New York, NY. Retrieved from https://digitallibrary.un.org/record/113822?ln=en.

UN. (1999). Violence against women in the family: Report of the Special Rapporteur on Violence Against Women, E/CN.4/1999/68. Retrieved from https://digitallibrary.un.org/record/271024?ln=en.

UN. (2002). Report of the Special Rapporteur on Violence Against Women, E/CN.4/2002/83. Retrieved from https://digitallibrary.un.org/record/459009?ln=en

UN. (2005). Report on Mexico produced by the Committee on the Elimination of Discrimination against Women under article 8 of the Optional protocol to the convention, and reply from the Government of Mexico, CEDAW/C/2005/OP.8/MEXICO. Retrieved from https://www.refworld.org/docid/4a54bc0e1a.html.

UN. (2012). Report of the Special Rapporteur on Violence Against Women, A/HRC/20/16. Retrieved from https://www.refworld.org/docid/5008088f2.html

UN. (2013). Agreed conclusions on the elimination and prevention of all forms of violence against women and girls. 57th session of the commission on the status of women, E/2013/27 E/CN.6/2013/11. Retrieved from https://www.un.org/womenwatch/daw/csw/csw57/CSW57_Agreed_Conclusions_(CSW_report_excerpt).pdf.

UN. (2016). Report of the Special Rapporteur on Violence Against Women, its causes and consequences. United Nations General Assembly, A/71/398. Retrieved from https://www.refworld.org/pdfid/5829cc9b4.pdf.

UNODC. (2019). *Global study on homicide 2019 (Booklet 5: Gender-related killing of women and girls)*. Vienna: UNODC.

Villa, E. N. R. M. (2020). *Circuito do feminicídio: O silêncio murado do assassinato de mulheres*. Rio de Janeiro: Lumen Juris.

Villa, E. N. R. M., & Machado, B. A. (2018). O mapa do feminicídio na polícia civil do Piauí: Uma análise organizacional-sistêmica. *Revista Opinião Jurídica*, 16(22), 86–107. doi:10.12662/2447-6641oj.v16i22

Weldon, L. S. (2002). *Protest, policy and the problem of violence against women: A cross-national comparison*. Pittsburgh, PA: University of Pittsburgh Press.

INDEX